The Writings of Satan

by
Brad Keating

Printed in the United States of America

ISBN 1-57558-001-2

In Dedication To:

The soon return of our Lord Jesus Christ. May He be
glorified as The King of Kings and Lord of Lords!

My Family:

My wife Natasha and our son, Elijah.
May our home be one of true Christian love; for the world,
for the family of God, and for ourselves.

I would like to express my deep appreciation to the following people for their contributions in writing and publishing this book:

Hugh Greer
Rob Lindsted, Ph.D.
Claire Lynn
Larry Lynn
Eric Lynn
Rebecca Lynn
Tim McNeal
Louise Meyer
Jackie Symons

Preface

Before my first book, "The God of the Jews Must Die" was published, I had two other books already in mind to write. When the first printing of "The God of the Jews Must Die" sold out, just months after it was published, I had the title "Tribulation Tragedy Part 1" added to the name for the second edition. I then began writing the sequel to my first book, with hopes that another view point of the tribulation might bring even more people to the Savior, Jesus Christ.

As with most sequels, much of this story is based upon the assumption that the reader has completed the first volume. Because of this, I did not repeat many of the horrors written in the previous book. Instead, I focused on the other events and thoughts that might occur during the same period of time in the tribulation.

With that in mind, I want to mention several aspects of the story before you begin. First, I do not endorse that the Anti-Christ or False Prophet named in the book must be the ones in the tribulation. The Bible gives many clues, but does not specifically name either one. The purpose of this book is to show the possible nature of their personalities based upon the Scriptures. It is my belief that their names will remain unknown until after the rapture.

Second, the story would be difficult to follow if an explanation was given for every action. It is my hope that the reader will use the Scriptures given in both books for a personal Bible study, along with other reference books. (A study guide of Scriptures is included at the end of the story. However, they are not given by chapters as in the first book, because many are either the same, mentioned specifically, or intertwined within the writing.) Finally, to write concrete ideas, where the Bible is abstract, leaves one open to criticism. By His wonderful grace, I believe the ideas and timetables expressed are as accurate as the Scriptures allow. Whether you agree or disagree with all of my ideas, please read this in the spirit in which it was written: to show the wickedness and deceitfulness of the Anti-Christ, and the love and glory of the true Messiah, Jesus Christ. I pray that this book will be used in helping Christians understand the tribulation, and using it for spreading the Good News. Even more, **I pray that if you haven't accepted Jesus Christ as your personal Savior, that you do so <u>before you put this book down</u>. Your life depends on it!**

The Beginning

My name is Joseph Van Buren the Third, the only child of Joseph and Catherine Van Buren of Vienna, Austria. My father was a member of Parliament for sixteen years, a conservative in the People's Party and director of the board for the Federal Bank. I was privately tutored until the age of eleven, then enrolled in military school, graduating with honors.

My years in military school, though spattered with an occasional whipping for general misbehavior, taught me personal discipline and body conditioning. Every day I devoted myself to running five miles, rifle shooting at the range and two hours of power lifting and muscle toning in the gymnasium. By graduation, my body had grown to six feet-four inches, and I could bench press almost five hundred pounds. I won the national championship in wrestling both my junior and senior years with perfect records. Many students and coaches encouraged me to continue my career in pursuit of Olympic competition, but destiny held another course for my life.

With much deliberation and parental consultation, I decided to serve my term in the Austrian armed forces. The army chose one hundred new recruits, of which I was one, to work in a specialized combat unit. We trained in every area of battle, but concentrated our skills for rescue missions and defensive government protection. I received top honors in marksmanship, personal combat, and fifth in explosive dismantling and detonation. We spent most of our time in the field practicing and working with the regular armed forces.

Of particular enjoyment to our units was the opportunity to freely pound on the new recruits in their protective gear, trying to knock them unconscious.

One time, a rather stout young man standing two inches taller then I, thought he could actually beat us in hand-to-hand combat. No one from the recruits could even touch him, so they appointed me to deflate his tender, but larger than life, ego. As I faced my adversary, I could hear my friends yelling about our unit's perfect record and the need of sustaining it, while he yelled about what he would do to me. My nostrils flared and I decided to end it as soon a possible. He made the normal error of pulling his rifle back to his right as I charged, but instead of using the bayonet from my left as we had been taught to kill the enemy, I threw my right forearm into his right temple with all my might wanting to teach him some respect. The thick helmet snapped off, while his head jerked to the right. His body crumpled to the ground in a heap as I landed on top, rolling next to him. An eerie hush fell over the onlookers as the sergeants ran over with smelling salts and water. Our unit burst into cheers as he wearily opened his eyes and shook his head. Triumphantly, I raised my fist in the air, daring anyone else to test their courage in fighting me.

I was contemplating a lifetime career in the military, when my father mentioned a possible position at the Federal Bank as a personal bodyguard for one of the richest men in the country. He told me that this man could end up being the next president, and with the European Economic Community going into effect in 1993, it was possible that he might be very influential in Europe. Since my father was a friend of Mister Hapsberg, he mentioned me as a candidate for the position of his bodyguard. He told him of all my credentials and training in the specialized combat unit. If I wanted the position, Mr. Hapsberg was willing to give me an interview. I had nothing to lose, so they set an appointment up during a break in my military schedule.

His office sat atop of the ten story bank, taking up almost half of the floor. Two armed guards stood aside the hand crafted, mahogany double doors, eyeing me suspiciously as the secretary led me into the office. Automatically from my years of training, I surveyed their weapons and body movements. Continuing my scrutinizing, I noticed the laser beam reflectors and what seemed to be an iron door that could swing shut protecting the office. A thick, thirty foot Asian carpet covered the marble floor leading to his desk. The walls were paneled with oak and beautifully arranged with plants and pictures of himself receiving awards. Golden ornaments were spread through-out the office and I saw several shaped into different types of animal heads. Around a corner, a conference room extended to the other side of the building. The long, mahogany table with fur-covered chairs, filled most of the room. An extra large president chair positioned at the head was obviously the place for Mr. Hapsberg to conduct the board meetings.

We walked up to his desk listening to him quote stock prices while he faced out the window. Spinning around, he hung up the phone and stepped around the desk to shake my hand. He walked with confidence, yet graceful like a king stepping down from his throne. His thick, dark hair was combed back and his light blue eyes seemed to almost twinkle as he flashed a big smile. Even though I was larger and stood two inches taller, he gave an aura of power from within his muscular frame that filled his silk, black suit. He spoke with a low, powerful voice, but it somehow soothed all my fears of being in his presence. The moment his forceful hand shook mine, I knew this was the man with whom my destiny lay.

SEVERAL YEARS LATER...

After being hired by the bank president, Mr. Hapsberg, several years ago, many events have changed this world of which I have been able to witness first hand. My job has mainly consisted of accompanying the President around Europe for his many business affairs. I sometimes work two weeks without a break while we travel out of the country, even sleeping in the same room on occasions.

The president (Mr. President is what I call him) was already in the process of developing a European currency when I was hired. With the iron curtain fallen and the United States on the decline, he worked hard with other countries to include them in the currency program. Shortly thereafter, the EEC officially started with the president playing an important role in negotiations on the currency exchange and trade deregulation. He truly felt that Europe would be the next and only superpower left on the planet.

The Rapture

The President phoned me early at home this September morning. "Sorry to call you so early, Joseph, but I need to meet you at the office at six-thirty," the President stated in an urgent voice.

"Yes, Mr. President, I'll be there," I answered. I heard the phone click on the other end. It had to be an emergency, I thought, he's never called me this early before.

Jumping out of bed, I rushed to take a quick shower and dress in my uniform. Usually, I only took my bullet-proof vest on trips out of the country, but the president's urgent call probably meant trouble. I grabbed my machine gun and two pistols while eating a granola bar and running to the stairs. My midnight-black Porsche roared out of the parking lot and onto the dimly lit street. Weaving in and out of the traffic, my mind raced with the possibilities for the president's call. We couldn't be rushing out of town because he did not ask me to pack. If the bank had been broken into, the police would've called me first. Maybe he wanted to fire me? No, that was not his style.

The security card opened the gate and I parked in my assigned spot in the nearly empty parking garage. The night cleaning crew glanced up with puzzled looks as I ran to the elevator, clutching my suitcase. Normally I enjoyed walking up the stairs to the top floor, but the elevator would be much faster. Stepping out of the elevator, I hurried towards the open doors into the President's office. His voice echoed from within the office as I tapped softly on the door. He acknowledged me with a glance and beckoned me to sit in my usual chair by his desk.

"It is perfect timing," he spoke into the phone. "Now listen to me, make sure the media continues to cover up the actual amount of people gone. I have already been in contact with the Russian, Chinese and Japanese govern-ments. The other heads of state are calling throughout the world...I know...distort the true numbers missing. This is our big chance to finally blame the United States and vault ourselves into number one. The time to act is now, we must be bold! Good...fine...Okay, see you tomorrow."

He hung up the phone with an unusual grin of satisfaction across his face. In the three years working for him, I could sense most of his moods. For the most part, he either had a smile that could brighten anyone's day, or an emotionless stare of deep concentration. Occasionally, a frown of determination developed if something did not work as he had planned. This was a new expression I had never seen.

"Have you heard the news?" He asked with his grin broadening to a smile.

"No sir, What news?" I replied.

His smile vanished as he began explaining the event of the night before. "Around one this morning, millions of people disappeared without a trace. Every country has at least some missing, but the United States was hardest hit. We don't know how many are missing from Europe, but the governments are limiting the media's reports so as not to alarm the rest of the world.

A buzz interrupted our conversation as he picked up the phone. "Thank you, Hello...Tell him that the President of the United States has been informed...Good...Good. We want the media to portray the great devastation in America. Yes. We also had several Americans with extended visas, they understand the situation. I'm waiting for their call...wait, there's another line. It's probably them. Call me later. Hello... Now get this straight: Tell your newscasters to concentrate on the United States. An occasional story from here is fine, but make sure they portray them as isolated incidents. Your head will roll if the EEC is shown in any sort of disarray. Don't worry, every one of my satellite stations are doing the same...CNN has been taken care of, they are under strict control. They'll do a better job for us in America anyway. Yes...Okay."

The president hung up the phone laughing. "Americans can be so gullible." He snickered.

"Sorry for the interruptions," he continued. "The time is now here. Europe is destined to rule the world as before, and I will be their man to lead us to world supremacy. Joseph, are you ready to go with me?"

"I...I don't think I understand, sir." I stumbled, staring inquisitively.

"We'll have time to discuss everything later," he assured. "But first, let me discuss my personal proposal to you. I know you can be trusted and have served the bank well over the last few years. Your father's boasting was right! However, I will be very busy for the next seven years or so and will need one person to supervise my protection. This person will be with me night and day, probably not able to take a vacation. There will be five other personal bodyguards and numerous others to coordinate. There will be much publicity along with great personal risk attached to this position. Whoever accepts this office will be a millionaire in seven years, with a home of his choosing anywhere in the world. He will also have the best of everything this world can offer, including his own servants. Joseph, my trusted servant, will you be this man?"

His eyes twinkled and teeth glistened as he flashed the smile that had won over everyone's heart. How could I resist the man? I knew he would go to the top when I met him. His aura of self-confidence and his warm personality gave me a sense of comfort. His economic empire and political clout is rising faster than an erupting volcano. The wealth and power I will have from this man will bring great personal security all the rest of my life. My destiny was with this man.

"Yes sir! I am ready to do whatever you ask." I exclaimed enthusiastically.

"That's great. I knew you would. I want you to go home today and have some fun. Pack one bag of whatever personal belongings you want to keep with you, but don't worry about clothes, regular necessities or food. My servant staff will be yours, to attend to any need you have. I want you to concentrate on me and nothing else. Tomorrow, report in at seven in the morning. The five other guards will be here and we will go over what I want and expect. Beginning tomorrow, you will remain with me at all times to protect from any attack, unless I specially tell you otherwise. Everything else will be written down for you tomorrow. Do you have any questions?"

"I have only one question if I may, Mr. President, but it doesn't reflect upon the position." I answered.

"Go ahead."

"Sir, what happened to all the people that disappeared, and why?"

"God has taken all the nuisances out of this world," he answered with a confident glare, "so that we would not be hindered any longer!"

The Power

The first day of my new seven year assignment for the president was uneventful and very tedious. I met with the five guards chosen to work under my supervision, spending the afternoon laying ground rules for our employment. The president lectured us on all the duties to be performed and warned of the various perils in our service for him. Afterwards, we all sat down to a catered meal from one of his favorite restaurants in Vienna, building camaraderie amongst ourselves.

Bidding farewell to the new bodyguards, the president brought me back to his home in one of his white limousines. The iron gates opened after a moment of identification by the security camera at the entrance. Oak, pine and spruce trees stood majestically over the driveway, giving a feeling of passing through a tunnel. Four large pillars towered at the top of the steps leading into the seventeenth-century mansion.

Once inside, the president excused himself to do further business, ordering his chief servant to tour the house with me. Every room was laden with gold and silver vessels decorated with diamonds, emeralds and rubies. Ancient paintings hung throughout the hallways, many of which pictured angels flying through the air. One particular painting that caught my eye sat atop the doorway leading out of the main entranceway. It depicted a goat head on a man's body. The human hands held a crystal ball into which the eyes of the goat stared. Horrible creatures flew around the room where the goat-man stood, all looking intently into the crystal ball. From within the ball, glowing eerily were the numbers six hundred sixty six.

The chief servant brought me into the room underneath the painting. "This is the president's worship room. Do not touch anything here," he cautioned.

Stepping through the doors, I could feel a cold chill creep up my spine as if there were invisible beings present in the room, watching my every move. Two small chandeliers hung on each of the four solid oak walls enclosing the dimly lit room. The ceiling was at least twelve feet high and the room was about fifty feet long and wide. Four tables full of hundreds of candles stood in each corner. Dozens of paintings depicting animal sacrifices, with angels and gruesomely ugly creatures participating, adorned the walls. Drawn in the middle of the floor was a five-pointed star enclosed by a circle.

"Why are there no chairs?" I asked with a puzzled look.

"I do not know," he responded. "The president often brings dignitaries and other...well, let's say...strange men for hours at a time in here. He calls it his personal worship room."

We walked out of the room into the warmth of the entry way, while the servant carefully closed the doors behind us. He nervously looked around, checking to see if anyone could hear.

He tugged on my shoulder, whispering in my ear, "Sometimes I hear screams from inside that room. There are low voices that I've never heard before." He continued cautiously, "I think they're demons!"

Approaching footsteps caused him to jump back and loudly say, "Now I will show you the master's living quarters."

We walked up the semi-circular marble staircase to the second floor. Trophy cases and metal suits from the crusades stood prominently on either side of the hallway. Several chandeliers hung from the ceiling, illuminating the glass cases. At the end of the hall, two solid oak doors led into the president's sleeping room.

"This is the master's bed and you will be sleeping in that room over there," the servant said.

Elegant antique gold, porcelain and carved wooden artifacts filled every wall and corner of the President's room. The tapestry-covered bed and all the chairs looked at least two hundred years old, but were in perfect condition. One large picture window rose from the floor to the top of the vaulted ceiling, revealing the flower gardens and patio in the back. The entry way of my room was of normal size, but there was no door or door frame, as if it were intended to be a guard room. My room was smaller and not nearly as lavish as the master bedroom, but the beautiful view of the back was just as spectacular.

"Sir, please put your belongings where you wish and fill out the papers on the table as soon as possible. They are questions about your measurements for clothes, favorite foods and other personal preferences. We will have your night clothes ready within the hour and a new wardrobe by morning. The president has breakfast served on the patio at 6:30 and will be expecting you to join him. At what hour would you like for me to awaken you?" The servant questioned.

"Let's see...My morning run, calisthenics, a shower. Oh about five would be fine. But I can use an alarm clock!" I answered, not wanting to be a nuisance so early.

"No sir, that will not be necessary. We will wake you quietly and open the drapes so as not to disturb the president," he replied. "Please relax until the president returns."

With that he showed me the bar and television controls, nodding politely as he walked out of the room.

About twenty minutes later, the president returned with his usual smile and took me to his office.

"We will not be home much anymore, but when we are, you may relax and enjoy the pleasures of my home," the president explained. "You need not worry about my safety within the confine of my estate. We are totally protected."

"Yes, sir." I replied.

After showing me the week's upcoming schedule, he told me to go relax in the hot tub before turning in for the evening. Not needing any further encouragement, I thanked him and excused myself for my first night in my new home.

Relaxing in the Jacuzzi which resembled a swimming pool, I thought about the great fortune fate delivered me: a luxurious home with servants attending my every whim; the best food money could buy; traveling the world in a Lear jet and limousines. And best of all, working for one of the kindest and most powerful men in all of Europe. I had reached the top! My dreams had come true.

The following afternoon, the President of Austria arrived at the bank. He was several inches shorter than my boss, with dark hair and fair skin. Like most politicians, he displayed perfect manners with a smile painted on his face. I always enjoy the reaction of people when my boss introduces me as a bodyguard. A menacing glare, coupled with my massive frame and weapons normally brings a stuttering response of nervousness. However, the Austrian President not only seemed unaffected by my presence, but acknowledged me like a friend. Whether his kindness was genuine or not, I could not tell, but I respected the effort.

Throughout the afternoon, they exchanged thoughts about the approaching meeting of the ten presidents. Phone calls were placed and received as my boss negotiated the political structure of a new alliance. Financial and marketing obligations were of high concern as well as how to bring my boss into the prominent position of leader over Europe. I carefully watched him as he handled all the questions and problems brought up. He seemed to have an answer for everything without even a hint of concern or anxiety. At the end of the day, the Austrian President accompanied us back to the mansion for dinner.

Around eight that evening, a small man dressed in a cape with gold ornaments, came to the door. I asked the servant who he was.

"He comes for special meetings with the president in his worship room. Three others will also come, dressed in the same type of outfits," he replied.

"What is your name?" I asked the man, stepping up in front of him.

The hood over his head covered everything except his wrinkled chin. He didn't so much as even twitch as I once again asked, "What is your name?"

Angrily demanding acknowledgment, I clenched my fists in front of my chest. The president's calming voice spoke from behind me, "It's okay, Joseph, thanks for being concerned."

"Yes, Mr. President," I stated. "I was just concerned for your safety."

"I know you were," the President assured me with a smile, "But I told you to relax here in the house. My servants know who is welcome and who is not."

"Yes, sir," I sheepishly replied, not sure if I had made a fool of myself.

Without a word to the man, the president escorted him to the worship room. He followed the president without a word or a glance, unaffected by my words and actions. The other three men came just a few minutes later, all acting in similar fashion. I watched as the Austrian President followed the final man into the room, closing the doors behind them. The eerie painting of the goatman seemed to be looking straight down into my eyes.

Why weren't any of these men even the slightest bit afraid of my presence? For the last six years my presence had struck fear into the hearts of all who met me. Even when some outwardly showed courage, their eyes betrayed their inward fear. All five of the men I met today were unafraid of my intimidating size. It was as if they thought I could not harm them.

A piercing scream from inside the worship room broke my train of thought. Instinctively, I rushed to the door, but hesitated to pull it open. The deepest voice I had ever heard spoke slowly from within the room.

"The time is now. Our hour is come. The way is paved, just as the Master has predicted. The other six chosen ones are ready, they will give you their power. The other three wait for the appropriate time. Our new man is in the Vatican, he has been setting the stones in place. Your pathway is clear. Do as the Master has prepared for you."

"But, why can't we enter into him?" Another low voice interrupted.

"Because he is a chosen vessel for the Master himself. No being may enter into the Prince without immediate and eternal punishment," the first voice replied.

"What shall be done about the media?" The president's familiar voice said.

"The Master has it in control." The voice replied, "They will hearken to your words. More will be foretold later, as the Master conveys His intentions. We must now depart and attend to urgent business. Praise be to our god!"

I backed away from the door, as the voice ceased talking with another piercing scream. Hastening up the steps, I walked into the bedroom. For the first time since my early days of school, trepidation swept over my shaking body. What had I committed myself to? Maybe this was more than I could handle. No, I assured myself, this is what the army trained me for. Why would I even think of being afraid of some old men and a mere Austrian President?

The Appointment

The five bodyguards surrounded the president as he quickly stepped out of the limousine. I followed close behind, watching the cameramen and photographers carefully. News people shouted question after question at the president about his intentions with all of Europe.

"I'm sorry, but I will not be able to answer until after the summit meeting," he replied to every question. "But I will spend time after the meetings to respond to all of you."

We stepped into the Berlaimont building in Brussels, home of the EEC for many years. The crowd could still be heard yelling outside the glass doors as the police blocked the stairs. Two of us walked on either side of the president to the opened elevator.

Ten men seated around a large circular table, turned towards us as we entered the room. The President of Austria nodded to me and glanced towards a chair next to the door. I took my seat, carefully scanning the entire room for explosives or other foreign devices. All the men stood up and shook hands with the president. He smiled and acknowledged each man by name and country.

The French President spoke in fluent English, "Gentlemen, as we have already discussed, the time is now here for Europe to take it's rightful place as ruler of the world. We know that total unification is the only answer to the pressing problems upon us. The world is now waiting for us to lead them down the road of economic prosperity. Each of us can take our rightful places in this new kingdom, but we must have a leader that will not be recognized as a threat to any country. I believe it is time to make official our total unification with the announcement of our new leader."

Everyone nodded in approval.

He continued, "I know all of us agree that Mr. Hapsberg should become our new head of power. His expertise in the economic revival of our countries through the new monetary system should enable us to dominate world affairs. He possesses the charisma that is needed to win all people, from each of our countries, over to this new union. He is already known for his work in global unity, environmentalism and his past record is impeccable. I need not say more about his qualifications. Without further ado, I would like to motion that we nominate Mr. Hapsberg as the official President of unified Europe."

"I second the motion," the Italian President confirmed.

"All in favor?"

"Aye," replied all ten men.

"All opposed?"

No one even twitched a muscle.

Turning to my boss, the French President said, "You now have total control of this meeting and all of Europe. May I be the first to congratulate you?"

The French President smiled and bowed his head towards the new President of Europe.

"Thank you all very much for my nomination," Mr. Hapsberg exclaimed. "We have much to discuss. First, the news media is already dubbing the new leader of Europe as the Prince. So as not to cause confusion and comply with our ally, please refer to me as Prince and I can acknowledge all of you as the Presidents. I feel this will help in our world media persona. Next, we need a name to indicate to all nations that we are a unified body. I would like to propose that we adopt the new name of The Federation. The media will pick up on this and help us to dissolve the problem of individual country identification. Any comments or discussion on this subject?"

"I think it is a great idea, Prince," the Grecian President exclaimed.

Everyone nodded in approval.

"All in favor?"

"Aye," chorused the ten men.

"All opposed?"

Again, no one uttered a sound.

"My next order of business deals with the new proposed Federation currency. We have been using the system on a voluntary basis, but I think we should pass into law its total usage. We have already begun hooking other countries into the system through my bank's computers. If nations refuse to comply, I will shut down their transactions in our computer system and they will be brought to a standstill. The American dollar will finally be abolished as the world's standard of money. Our Federation currency will be the only world standard!" The Prince said enthusiastically.

"We have long awaited this opportunity," the Belgium Prime Minister stated. "I think we all agree that this is the time to make it official."

Everyone nodded in approval.

"All in favor?" The Prince asked.

"Aye," chorused the ten men.

"Any opposed?"

Once again, no one dared to utter a sound.

"As everyone has received in the faxes I have sent," The Prince continued as if the voting process were just a formality. "I think the total unification of our military power is a top priority. By the plans that you already received, I believe we can achieve Super Power status within weeks. Every country is included in the program and all have equal protection in the new plan. Each of you have given me your ideas and comments over the last week. This is the final plan I have developed using everyone's ideas.

The Prince passed out papers to each man.

"After talking with each of you, I felt the best man to head up the implementation of this plan would be the Spanish King, Juan Carlos. He should have the easiest time in creating a unified atmosphere for our troops."

The Prince stopped for a moment, looking at each man with a gleam in his eye. "Gentlemen, if we follow this plan, we will be the rulers of the entire world."

Grins of pleasure spread over each man's face.

"Does anyone have any questions about what is to take place?"

"I think we have already agreed that this is what needs to be done," the English Prime Minister stated.

"Go ahead and look over the papers to see if there are any questions on duties to be performed by each country," the Prince said.

I noticed a plane or helicopter approaching our building from the southern sky. I stood up to check on the unidentified object when my radio vibrated to warn me of an urgent message. I slipped my earphone on to hear the message from the army commander.

"Sir, we have an unidentified helicopter approaching the building that will not respond to radio identification. We are intercepting at this moment," he said.

The Prince watched me with a look of puzzlement while the other Presidents were absorbed in their material. Two Air Force choppers flew over the building directly at the approaching helicopter.

"Sir, we have identified the private helicopter. It was hired by American media to take pictures up close of the summit meeting."

"Take them down and lock them up until the Prince decides their fate." I commanded.

I nodded to the Prince, who had continued watching the event waiting for the outcome. He grinned with approval as I sat down at my reserved seat.

"Gentlemen, I would also like to mention the latest successes in our peace and economic treaties. I will be signing a new deal with Israel that will benefit us all. We will need their oil and agricultural products in the upcoming years. I am promising military support and products that each of our countries produce. With all the existing pacts in the Middle East, I believe it will be to our benefit to step up and sign both a military and economic treaty. I feel that a seven year deal will give us time to take control of what we need to assure our stability. The final preparations are being performed at this moment and I will leave for Israel shortly after our announcement of the Federation. Are there any questions concerning these latest developments?"

"Do we have any other treaties or pacts on the drawing board since you last spoke to us?" the Spanish King asked.

"As we discussed before, all individual agreements made by our members here in the past, must be sanctioned by the Federation to show our unification. However, any and all negotiations in which I partake as President of the Federation must be voted passage. Before I would negotiate any other treaties, everyone in this room will be notified. However, I assure you, that all my foreign dealings will be to only strengthen the Federation's position of world dominance.

Hundreds of thousands of spectators jammed the streets while hundreds of millions more watched the live report of the Prince making the official announcement of the forming of the Federation. The crowds cheered as he announced this troubled time as a new beginning of world peace and prosperity. The media heralded the Federation President as the new "Prince" of Europe with strong voices of affirmation to the hopes portrayed by the rising leader. No one criticized any word he spoke, for his confident speeches filled them with optimism, and a reason to expect a better world through global peace.

My hands were full trying to keep the reporters and admirers away from the Prince. Everyone wanted either a picture or just to touch him. Even when I became frustrated endeavoring to keep away the ignorant, pushy people, the Prince, always spoke in kind, comforting words. He absolutely forbade me to hurt anyone, especially members of the media, which I desired so greatly to punch.

"The media is our tool of prominence," the Prince would say. "Without them, we cannot win the hearts of the world."

I am beginning to realize my purpose for the Prince is to be a buffer zone between his warm personality and getting places we need to go. By himself, the Prince stands taller and broader than the other Presidents of the Federation, causing others to feel intimidated by his presence. However, when I stand next to the Prince, I give the aura of power, allowing him to be seen as non-threatening. I also am the one who pushes our way through the crowds and gets the Prince where he wants to go, portraying me as the harsh one and him the approachable, kind leader who is being led to his next meeting as if he didn't really want to go. I must admit, it works great and I don't mind at all. I like having the license to push and be rude to others in our way, though I would like to show some of them an ex-military punch or two.

The other five bodyguards spend their time helping me get through the crowds, and searching for any type of weapon that might be used against the prince. So far, no one has attempted to harm him or disrupt any meeting due to the overwhelming acceptance of his leadership of the Federation. The world has a new leader.

The Treaty/Day One

"That's right, I will finance the buy out. The city of Babylon is going to be my crown jewel," the Prince expressed with a smile as he hung up the mobile phone. He looked out the window of his private jet, and down at the vast Mediterranean Sea below.

"Please get the Austrian President on the phone for me," the Prince politely asked his secretary.

"Right away, sir," she replied.

Grabbing his calculator and pen, he began writing on papers sprawled across the desk in front of him. I leaned back in my recliner shutting my eyes, thinking about visiting Jerusalem for the first time. I had heard so many stories about the ancient holy city. Could it possibly be as great as the many religious leaders thought?

"I have him for you," the secretary said to the Prince in a soft voice, not wanting to disturb his concentration.

"Thank you," the Prince replied. "Mr. President, I wanted you to be the first to know of my final buy out of Babylon. I will be signing all the papers when I return to Vienna. Austria will get the first choice of location as promised. Uh huh. Yes. We are already sending location engineers to obtain preliminary plans for the first market area. We should begin actual building early next month. They will use the existing reconstruction with the new layout for the quickest route to opening. I informed them that time is of greatest importance, because we will need the support of as many countries as possible. We will push for early commitments to Babylon in order to obtain extra construction funds, so as not to constrain all my resources. Good. After we receive the first renderings by the architects, we'll send them off in a preliminary media exposure. Okay, I'll call after the meetings in Israel. Bye."

The Prince handed the phone back to his secretary and continued his calculations while the plane descended into Israel.

As the limousine weaved it's way through the crowded streets, my mind contemplated past experiences of thousands of years ago. I could not get over the feeling of the historical significance of Jerusalem or the many mysteries of its spiritual richness in several religions. The famous King Solomon and his great wealth resided in this town. King David who brought the Jews their great fame fought many wars here. The great leader of the Muslim religion, Mohammed, rose into the heavens and spoke with God from the hill on which the Dome of the Rock stands. Of course, the great leader of the Christian religion, Jesus Christ, was crucified just outside the city limits.

I find it interesting that the religion most traumatized by the disappearance of a couple of weeks ago was Christianity. Though many Christian churches still remain, very few if any other religions were affected. The Prince and most other leaders claim it is due to the piousness and lack of world harmony amongst those who disappeared. He says those who are open-minded and progressive were left to prosper and encourage those here on earth. I wonder, though, why would the Jewish nation be affected so little by the disappearance if the prophet Jesus Christ is the pillar of Christianity?

The limousine eased in front of the steps to the Knesset building surrounded by tens of thousands of onlookers. Two of the bodyguards checked through the crowd looking for any sign of trouble. After their approval, I stepped out of the limousine to the bright television lights and many camera flashes of the photographers. Everyone in the world was tuned to the monumental peace and economic treaty-signing between the Federation and Israel. The Prince emerged following close behind, smiling and waving to the crowd. We made our way through the thronging crowds up the steps into the building.

The Israeli Prime Minister and President met with the Prince for several hours that afternoon. Each man discussing the primary points of importance in the forthcoming treaty. The Prince promised military support if formally requested by the Israeli government. He also mentioned the possibility of shared troop support, just as the European nations have done in the forming of the Federation. The Federation and Israel would exchange the same amount of soldiers for training and general duties. The Prime Minister and President agreed to look into that possibility in the near future. They also expressed their concern of unnecessary pressure for conformity in any religious practices, but the Prince assured them of his personal backing in their freedom of worship.

The following day, the Prince addressed the world. "With the power vested in me by the Federation, I have come not only to confirm the existing Middle East treaties, but to announce a new economic and military pact between Israel and our nations. We feel the recognizing of Israel's agreements in the Middle East is an important step in world peace. It is my personal goal to bring all the countries of the planet into a fully peaceful unity. In addition, we want to provide economic growth for both parties in our economic plan. I take this opportunity to appeal to the people and governments of all nations to join in a new World Order. The Federation is in a financial and military position to work with all countries in building a better future for our planet. However, we must unite together in a New World Order to focus on one purpose...It's time for World Peace!"

The excited crowd broke into cheers as the Prince shouted his final words thrusting his hand into the air with the familiar peace sign of his two fingers. Standing next to him in amazement, I stared at his majestic figure silhouetted against the bright blue sky. He really will bring world peace I thought to myself.

Day 28

During this last month I have seen more of the world than most people will in their lifetime. Everyday, in a different city, the Prince speaks about global unity. Between speeches there are meetings, banquets and business deals to attend. He speaks on the phone for hours at a time, arranging new business and government deals around the world. He often goes days with only short one hour catnaps as his only time of rest. I've asked him several times if he thinks he should take a day off to rest and relax. He always stares at me for a moment, seemingly searching my intent, then smiles and explains the time is short. I'm just thankful he allows me to sleep on the jet, so I can stay rested to protect him elsewhere!

Descending into Rome, I watched the brilliant orange sunset over the famous seven hills of the city. The upcoming conference of all the top religious leaders could make or break the possibility of world peace. If people could somehow be joined in religion, almost all of the racial and ethnic heritage wars would cease. For this reason, the Prince worked closely with the Pope in arranging this conference of religions. Many of the phone calls they made to each other sounded as if they were collaborating together as strategists rather than as separate political and religious powers. As we walked off the plane, a crowd of people filled the area between the terminals and into the parking lot. Many held signs welcoming the Prince and supporting his mission for world peace. The tens of thousands of admirers broke into screams as the Prince stepped out behind me. He waved nonchalantly to everyone, standing at the top of the steps to smile for all the cameras and pictures. Fortunately, the police were prepared for the huge crowd and we were able to pass to the waiting limousine with only an occasional stop for autographs and handshakes. I began contemplating the problems ahead for crowd control when we met the Pope and the others. Who knows how many would show up for this spectacular religious extravaganza?

The Prince continued his preparations for the meeting while the limousine drove through the streets of Rome. He was working with his laptop computer, jotting down last minute notes when the phone buzzed. "Sir, the Pope wishes to speak to you," the chauffeur said.

"Thank you," he replied picking up the phone. "Hello. Yes. Is everything prepared? Good. Yes. They're already there? Excellent. I have many instructions for the leaders. They should receive enough authority for each one of them to agree. Of course, I know some of the media is saying I am doing it to have control of the World Religion. I don't think it will be a problem. With the final explanation of the disappearance and the push for world peace, we should have no trouble controlling the few opponents. No. Good. If we do have problems with a few of the independent stations, I already have men set up to begin the slander campaign. Yes, that is a concern. It will take time to win over everyone to our side, but our Father has it under control. Okay, make sure we keep our distance. If any of the leaders suspect anything on our part, it may throw a wrench into the proceedings. Okay. Bye."

"Joseph," the Prince said looking at me.

"I want to warn you of the huge crowds awaiting us," the Prince said. "There is a lot of concern about the religious zealots and their possible attempts to interrupt the conference. I am safe here, but please help watch for any signs of trouble involving any of the other leaders."

"Yes sir," I said.

"I don't mean to add any more pressure on you, but I know you will do better than all of the police assigned to the task of protection."

"No problem, sir." I confidently replied.

"Good. Thank you. Again, I am safe here, so don't worry about me these next few weeks," the Prince stated.

Sir, I can do both without forsaking my first obligation to you." His smile and slight nod of approval revealed his pleasure in my reply. We pulled up behind another limousine in front of the Vatican. I saw a bearded, elderly gentleman, dressed in a white robe, step out and hurry past the throngs of people reaching over the police barricades trying to touch him. There were so many people surrounding the limousine, I could not even see the building.

"Walk slowly this time, Joseph," the Prince said.

"Ah, yes sir." I answered with a puzzled look.

Noticing this, the Prince explained, "None of the religious leaders are acknowledging the crowd because of their fear of some fanatical harassment. I want to show them my patience, love and lack of concern for physical harm. If they see me as one who cares about all people and has no interest in religious barriers, they will be more open to religious unification."

"Yes sir, I understand."

The crowd went into hysteria as the Prince stepped out smiling and waving to the people. Instead of racing through the waving crowds as the others had, he slowly walked down the pathway, trying to touch every outstretched hand. He even smiled and greeted some of the police who were trying to stand in the barricade. As the crowd sensed the Prince's friendliness, they began to push against the police line. Finally, the human barricade collapsed around us while everyone tried to touch the Prince.

The Prince grabbed the back of my uniform and stated with a laugh, "Okay, now you can get me into the building!"

Taking my cue, I started shouting at the mob, stretching my forearms in front of me. I used my strength to push everyone in my path out of the way. Breathing a sigh of relief, we entered the doors.

"Good job," stated the Prince, still laughing. "This will be fun to watch on television tonight."

The meetings were long and boring to me--all these puffed up religious leaders trying to explain how important their religion was.

We only listened to about one-forth of the group for each of the first four days. Everyone shared ideas on how to incorporate their practices into the benefit of all. Then the Prince began bargaining in his normal, slick fashion, trying to persuade each leader to agree to the overall plan, using a part of each religion. The two most powerful leaders, the Pope and the spokesman for the New Age movement continued to bicker and vie for the lead role in the World Church. After two weeks of meetings, I was beginning to think it would be impossible for everyone to actually pull together for religious unity.

"Get the Pope on the phone for me, please," the Prince asked on our way to the Vatican for the third week of the summit. "Joseph, be on the watch today."

"Yes sir," I replied, knowing something was amiss. He had spent an unusually long evening with his priests in prayer the night after they arrived from Austria. He had rented an entire floor in one of the hotels just for us and the priests.

"He's on the line, sir," the driver exclaimed.

"Great. Thank you," the Prince answered. "I've finished the preliminary by-laws for the Church. Everyone has a part in it, plus the freedom to do their own practices inside the Church. Yes. Yes. Right. Continue playing the Master's advocate. It will be the best way. Of course. I think everyone feels you will be the biggest opponent and will not be swayed easily. Yes. Keep it up. Okay. The Master's blessings be upon you."

The revealing of the by-laws for the World Church proved to be the break through in the discussions. Each leader seemed to be pleased with his part in the plan. However, the Pope voiced his concern of leaving some of the traditional values for these new ideas. The meetings broke for lunch with the Pope finishing his lecture on tradition. The room slowly emptied of the leaders and their personal interpreters which they had brought, although most of them spoke fluent English as well as their native language.

The Prince stepped over to the New Age leader and asked, "Would you please join me at my table today for lunch?"

"Yes, I will do that," he answered.

We sat down together with another New Age leader in the main dining hall. Because of the Prince's warning I continued watching for any signs of trouble, but nothing unusual was happening.

"I think I know how to persuade the Pope to follow the practices being sought by the World Church," the Prince said, folding his hands thoughtfully in front of him while staring into the eyes of the man.

"What is your idea?" the New Age leader questioned curiously.

"It seems clear to me now that we will be adopting most of your religion's convictions, even though Catholicism will have it's freedom. If we can adopt these by-laws we have written, you will always be known as the man who had the influence. We both know that the Christ will soon be revealed and He would be very pleased with your dealings if we could unify the church before he came."

"Yes, what you say is true," he agreed.

"We also need a headquarters for the World Church with the most well known person in the world as the spokesman," the Prince stated with a pause.

"I agree, do you think the Pope should be the spokesman?

The Prince leaned back in his chair with the smugness of victory written in his eyes which I had seen many times before. "You have the same thoughts, I see."

"I know that either he or myself would be the logical choice, since we have the two richest and most powerful religions."

"If we can persuade the Pope to the new way of thinking, while promising his traditions, we would capture a billion devoted followers into the World Church!" the Prince exclaimed enthusiastically. "Without the Vatican as headquarters, or the Pope as the spokesman, I'm afraid we could never achieve the spiritual or financial backing of his followers. I know he would agree to sharing the Vatican with you or some other chosen leaders to use as the center for the World Church."

After a few moments of silence, the New Age spokesman responded. "What you say is good. We should try to convince the Pope to conform to the new ways."

Two of the Pope's Palatine guards came to our table and asked for the Prince to accompany them to the Pope's private room. The Prince nodded and said, "Wish me luck. Joseph, please escort the others to the conference room for me."

"Yes sir," I replied.

We stood up from the table as the Prince walked out with the other two guards. It was the first time the Prince had been guarded by anyone but myself.

A few minutes after the Prince had left, a man dressed in a colorful robe stepped through the door and shouted, "No one move! I have a bomb attached to me!"

The entire banquet room hushed as he ripped his robe off revealing the shoulder harness with the bomb attached. "I am the Christ! But you did not invite me to the conference. How dare you not include the Christ of Divine Appointment into the World Church!"

I sat about fifty feet away with no obstructions between us. Slowly, I lifted my hand gun into my lap, carefully scrutinizing his every movement. His head moved from side to side to watch the entire room as he continued shouting doctrine. Checking the wall behind him, I knew I would have just a split second to aim and fire. Even with my years of training, my heart raced knowing one wrong move would bring my demise. He turned his head to shout his next rehearsed line of religious self proclamation to the stunned room. With split-second timing, I pointed to his open ear and pulled the trigger. As his head snapped back, I leaped toward him like a tiger jumping on its prey, hoping to shield some of the shrapnel if it was an impact detonation explosive. I closed my eyes as his body slumped to the ground falling onto his right arm. Screams from some of the waitresses pierced my ears, but nothing exploded in my face.

Everyone jumped behind tables to take cover, as I kneeled down to dismantle the bomb. Automatically I began the process, so familiar from my years in the army. Sweat drops rolled down my cheeks as I wished I had studied to be first in dismantling explosive devices in military contests. Moments later, the life cord to the explosive was cut and I breathed a sigh of relief.

"Okay, it's safe!" I proclaimed standing back up. I was covered with blood and sweat poured from my forehead into my eyes.

The crowd began cheering while I moved out from behind their cover. A waiter with a table cloth stepped up and placed it over the self-proclaimed Christ. Palatine guards rushed in wondering what had transpired. I gave them precise instructions on how to dispose of the bomb and left to shower back at the hotel room.

The conference took a turn that afternoon upon the Prince's announcement of the Pope's willingness to work with the New Age and a combined doctrine. The Prince laid out plans of how to use the Vatican as the Spiritual center, along with the purpose of new spiritual centers around the globe. Everyone seemed to agree with the idea of the Pope as the official spokesman for the new World Church. The rest of the week would be spent debating and adopting the written by-laws.

Later at the hotel, I questioned the Prince. " Sir, you seemed like you knew about the man with the bomb."

He smiled and questioned back, "If I had known exactly what would take place this afternoon, do you think I would take a chance of losing my best bodyguard?"

"But you were out of the room just before it happened... and you didn't take me...like you wanted me there for it," I stammered.

"Joseph," the Prince chuckled, then reassuringly said, "I told you that I was safe here in Rome, but that doesn't mean everybody's safe. You are the best protection here, now everybody knows it. Enjoy the glory!"

His words exhorted me as I remembered the cheering crowds and television interviews. Even the Pope commended my bravery, presenting me with a solid gold cross. Yet, the Prince never answered my question. Could he really know the future?

Day 284

"I just got the news after getting off the plane," the Prince explained into the limousine phone. We were driving through the streets of Washington D.C. "After my speech with the President I will call the General about his ideas. No, I see no reason to help Israel if they don't ask for it. I'm sure they are preparing for Russia's attack. I won't risk any of our troops if we don't have to. Yes, I agree. If I make any moves, it might portray me as leaving our stand of World Peace. We must remain neutral as long as possible. Yes, I talked with the Pope yesterday and he says all is going well with the building of the new Spiritual Centers. Everyone clung to our explanation of the disappearance as God removing those who would hinder our next step of World Peace and unification. My coined phrase "The New Beginning" brings feelings of solutions instead of questions. Our reports show that most people have forgotten about the incident and think the media hyped the event for ratings. Yes, just as we planned. Covering up the true amount of missing people really helped in bringing the world's view of America's prominence to fall far below the Federation. Yes. No. I already did. I think both civil wars in Korea and the Philippines will be drawing to a close. Africa is so hot with fighting I wouldn't touch it. Yes, I am going to commend the United States for trying to end the wars in Central and South America. Okay. Talk to the other nine Presidents. Let's continue working towards adopting the

World Church as the official religion. It will take some time. Fine. Bye."

I listened intently to the Prince's conversation with the Austrian President. Over seven months ago, after the Pope's first broadcast of the World Church, I thought unification was just around the corner. The unexpected eruption of riots in the last three and a half months quickly dampened my expectations, even though the Federation has remained unscathed by any fighting! We continue to prosper economically and our new military strength grows tremendously each day with the influx of new troops from the ten nations. The Prince labors tirelessly, traveling to many countries, pushing his World Peace campaign. Right now, he isn't receiving much support.

"Sir, the Spanish King is on the phone," the driver interrupted.

"Thank you," the Prince answered. "Hello, General. Yes, I just heard. I was going to call you after my speech here in America. I know. I figured with their poor harvest and continued economic struggles, it was inevitable that Russia would move to capture Israel's growing supplies. I know that Iraq, Jordan, Egypt, Libya, Turkey, Ethiopia and some of the Baltic states are planning to join forces in the assault. What? I do not think there is any way to reason with the Russian president. Ever since his election, he has uttered words of war. No way. If Israel doesn't ask, we will not give them military support. I will try some economic sanctions, but Russia is so far under I don't think it will matter. Go ahead. Yes. Keep as many troops in Babylon as you feel are necessary. I don't want anything to hinder the construction. We have too much money at stake to take a chance. I've already talked to him about our troops in Babylon. He understands and will cooperate fully. Good. Well, let's just say if Russia succeeds, it will eliminate many future problems. However, what can't be accomplished through war...can be accomplished through peace!"

Day 360

The Prince clapped his hands together triumphantly. He pressed the remote control button to turn off the television in his office. "That's it, Joseph," he chuckled. "We are the number one military power in the world!"

"What about Israel?" I questioned. "After what has happened, I don't think anyone can beat them."

"Ha. The Russians were stupid," he exclaimed. "There are times you use force, there are times you threaten force, and there are times when you befriend your enemies to achieve your objectives."

The intercom buzzed. "Sir, the Pope wishes to speak to you."

"Great. Thanks. Hello. Isn't it marvelous? The wars are all finished. I've heard as many as twelve million soldiers were killed. Only two million made it out of Israel alive. Yes, I think it would be a great idea. If you mention how Russia continued their denial of God, it would be a perfect opportunity to promote the World Church. Yes, I'm moving ahead with the plans to incorporate the World Church as the official religion of the Federation. I'm still having some opposition to the proposal. No. I think it will happen in the next few months. I'll keep you posted. Bye."

"Please get me through to the Israeli Prime Minister," the Prince said into the intercom.

"Thank you," the Prince stated after waiting a few moments. "On behalf of the entire Federation, we want to congratulate your country on its miraculous victory. Yes, I think it's wonderful to get the overwhelming support. To begin your sacrifices after such a stunning outcome will greatly strengthen moral support. Yes, yes. I give my full support and will schedule a visit shortly. No. There is one more item, please send a price to my secretary for grain and long term storage food items. I would like to support you with a buyout of any excess food and a contract for further purchases. No. Actually, we have already built several large storage facilities with more on the way. Yes, we'll settle it on Friday. Okay. Sure. I'll let you get back to your celebration. Once again, the Federation congratulates your entire country. Okay. Bye."

The Prince stood up form behind the desk, stepping over to the picture window overlooking the city. He laughed out loud while turning to look at me.

"Well, Joseph, they're beginning sacrifices to their God."

"Is that good, sir?" I questioned.

He turned back to the window. "It's better than good. Everything is going just as planned."

The intercom buzzed. "Sir, the Austrian President is on the phone."

"Thanks," the Prince answered. "Ahhh, my good friend. Didn't I tell you not to worry? Of course I'm right. Don't forget, we have power from the Master. I talked to Israel about their food and the United States has already agreed to our purchase price for the three years on their grain. Keep pushing the other President's to prepare. If they won't take a chance now, they'll pay dearly later. Trust me. How are they responding to my proposal of adopting the World Church? Not bad, but I think I will put an end to those three if they put up more stumbling blocks. Yes, we received two more bids for spots in Babylon. With the wars completely ended, I expect between ten to twenty bids over the next week. The grand opening is set for tomorrow at nine. Bye."

Smiling from ear to ear, the Prince gleefully hung up the phone. He picked up his pen and calculator, immediately punching in numbers.

I can't ever remember having seen him this joyous before. He seemed to be able to control the future, or at least predict what can happen. Is he using the supernatural forces to gain power and insight towards world events, or are they controlling him?

Day 540

The splendor of Babylon glistened under the midday sun. Each building was a picture of the full glory of modern architecture mixed with magnificent ancient stone sculpting. A seventy story skyscraper, like the head of a growing body, stood in the midst of the expanding transportation city carefully monitoring its every move. The best public transportation system ever devised, pushes visitors through like blood taking needed nutrients through the body, every location connected by the latest pollution-free electric buses and underground subways. The expansive airport, like human lungs, brings bodies in and out of the city like breaths of fresh air. The massive river ports, like a heart, pump new supplies from all over the world into the greatest marketplace ever designed. Babylon has become the perfect city, like a human body, created for optimum function if given the right instruction.

The Prince looked up to his seventy story crown jewel, crawling with construction workers hastily trying to finish the project. With a big smile, he leaned over and whispered, "We can see all of Babylon from my office on the top floor!"

"It is a spectacular sight," I replied with a hushed voice.

The announcer finished his introduction to the thousands gathered for the opening ceremony. "Now please give a hearty welcome to the man behind this great plan. The Prince!"

The crowds loudly cheered as the Prince stepped to the microphone. "Thank you. I'd like to welcome each and every one of you from all of your respective nations to our dreams of making money and improving the standard of living in all countries. At this time, almost every country has secured a place in this new trade city. Now, for the first time ever, we can come to one place, buy and sell products with no worries of fraud, exchange rates, or restrictions. Bring your goods to Babylon!" the Prince shouted.

The crowds broke into long applause with occasional chants.

"As everyone knows," the Prince continued, "this city is built for the buyers' convenience. It will be a shopper's paradise. Every part of the city has its function, and the transportation system is unparalleled. Federation troops, ships and aircraft will ensure safety for you and your goods. Not only will all the merchants of the world come to Babylon, it will also be a Mecca for individual consumers. We will all enjoy the pleasures this world offers!"

The Prince finished his speech with more words on the glories of Babylon, then we hopped into the limousine to take us back to the airport.

"Will this be your new headquarters, sir?" I asked.

"No, we will be coming here often, but I have other plans for a permanent headquarters," the Prince retorted.

"Does that mean we will be leaving Austria?"

"You will see, Joseph, you will see."

The waiting jet flew out of Babylon as soon as we were on board. I sat back in my familiar recliner, placing my order for dinner. The Prince promised to meet all of my necessities, but I almost felt guilty eating soup, salad and steak every day while the great famine approaches six full months around the globe. Most people throughout the world either scavenge for bites to eat or cut down to one small meal a day. Because of the Prince's foresight, we stocked up enough food supplies for the next ten years. The Federation presidents are making a lot of money following his explicit directions on buying supplies and signing long term trade agreements at very low prices.

"The Pope is on the phone, sir," the tall, blue-eyed secretary told the Prince. With her long blonde hair and cover-girl looks, it was amazing that he never seemed to give his secretary a second look. I know he could have any woman he wanted, but he just didn't show any interest in anyone. Maybe he thought it would hurt his reputation like so many other politicians in the past.

"Thank you," he answered. "Hello. Everything went great, thanks for asking. How are things in Rome? Great. No, we do not have full support of all the Presidents. The three from England, Belgium and Netherlands are adamantly opposed to forcing their nations into one religion. I'll give them some time to change their minds, then I'll take action. Let's see how quickly the other nations follow suit with accepting the World Church as the only religion. ....You are correct. There are so few that oppose the Church, I don't think they would interrupt anything, but I want total control so we can eliminate those who oppose. No, Israel is a special case, they haven't technically broken any laws, especially with the Spiritual Center right next to their new temple. Don't worry, your time will come. I'll call you after the worship. Okay. Bye."

I thanked the servant for my dinner and handed him my empty tray. Needing some rest, I closed my eyes while the Prince made another phone call. The lack of sleep overwhelmed me as the voices faded out.

The wrinkles of many years could not be hidden by the hood covering his face. His parched lips protruded out from the shadows, refusing to twitch even at my beckoning. The three priests always walked into the Prince's worship room in utter silence, almost in a trance.

"Don't worry about them, Joseph," the Austrian President reminded me. "They need total concentration for their prayers."

The Prince walked down the marble steps following the others into the room. I slowly inched over to the closed doors, pretending to guard them, as I strained to listen to what was said from within.

After about twenty minutes, just as I was ready to go back to my room for a bath, the slow, deep voice spoke as before. "You have done well for the Master. He is quite pleased at the progress being made. All is going as planned. There are problems ahead, but

I have come to speak the Master's desire. There are three men being prepared to replace those whose hearts have turned. You will know them when they bring your number before their steps. The time will be shown. Discontent is spreading through some countries. Prepare to use force in a peaceable way in bringing these objectors into submission. The Master has also informed me of a forth-coming event. There will be two enemies sent to Israel. Kill them if you can, but be cautious, as these are from of old and have much of the Enemy's spirit. Don't allow media exposure until we defeat them. The Master is coming soon! Prepare his way!"

The voice ended with a loud shriek from someone inside. Fear gripped my being. I spun around, bounding quickly up the steps to my room. My heart pounded in my chest. I sank down in my bed trembling in terror. I had never been afraid of any man, but I knew that the voice that spoke those words was not the voice of a man!

Day 720

"I told you to make sure all news reporters were pulled out of Jerusalem!" The Prince spoke in an exasperated, harsh tone. "Until we know what these two men are about, I don't want any coverage. It may hurt the morale of the nations right now. Okay, sounds good. If we can deceive the people into thinking they are like all the other nut cases, it may work to our advantage. We arrive in Jerusalem in a few minutes, I'll talk to you then."

"Joseph, did you replace the other bodyguard?" the Prince asked.

"Yes sir," I answered. "He will be ready to go when we arrive back in Austria. I put Matthew in charge of training him while we are away."

"Good job," the Prince said with a nod of approval.

The plague of death had taken my fellow bodyguard along with millions of others from around the world. It was difficult to see him robbed of life, especially with a great career ahead of him serving the Prince. I also lost one cousin to an attack of wild dogs, and another close friend from the military was murdered on the streets of Paris. Due to the plagues, murders, animal attacks and starvation, over one billion people have died in the last six months! The Pope has mentioned a time of testing in our next step of World Utopia. It's all a part of natural selection, he said, just like this planet has experienced for millions of years since God set everything in motion.

"Stay close by me until I know what to expect," the Prince stated.

"Yes sir," I replied.

The Prime Minister met us at the airport, immediately taking us to the new temple.

"I am pleased that you have come to see the temple and to tour the city again," the Prime Minister said.

"I am sorry it has taken so long to finally arrive. We have had many pressing problems around the world...as you know," the Prince stated.

"Oh yes, it is a changing world we live in," the Prime Minister replied.

"You know we continue full support of all that you do," the Prince started. "I would like to see more of an exchange program with our students and military. Your soldiers and officers are a great benefit to the Federation."

"Likewise the Federation's soldiers to our military, and we appreciate the interest of your students to the Jewish history and culture," the Prime Minister interrupted.

"Well," the Prince said laughing, "in my family tree, it seems we may have had some of Jewish descent, which has intrigued me for quite some time."

"Interesting," the Prime Minister said with his eyebrows raised. "Maybe that is why you have taken so kindly to our small nation."

"Probably, but I also have studied Israel's history and see it as a thriving nation after total destruction nineteen hundred years ago, I feel it a privilege and duty to do what I can for you. Though, as I mentioned before, we had hoped you would have officially asked for help against the Russians."

"But God had His purpose," the Prime Minister said. "Now we have united the religious and political opponents because of it."

"I hope to see a united political and religious world in the years to come," the Prince replied.

The car came to a sudden stop, interrupting the conversation.

"Prime Minister, I believe the two nut cases are right down that street," the chauffeur stated, motioning through the privacy window to a crowd gathered in the middle of the street.

We stepped out of the car and walked towards the throng of people spread across the street from sidewalk to sidewalk. Most of the onlookers were so intent on getting a glimpse of the two supposed preachers, they did not move out of our way. After repeated shouts to a man standing in front of me, my frustration overcame my congeniality, I picked him up by the arm and tossed him to the side. I then bulled my way to the front with the Prince, Prime Minister and other guards close behind.

"You must repent, O Israel," shouted one of the old men standing in the street. "The kingdom is coming! Prepare ye the way of the Lord!"

I snickered as I looked upon these two pitiful looking old men talking about God. Both were dressed in sackcloth, dirtied by ashes, looking as if they hadn't washed their clothes in months. Their clean hair and gray beards hung several inches below their necks, contrasting with the dusty robes. Each held a staff in his right hand, though they stood proudly upright with no help from the canes. As they continued, I found it odd that they were speaking in my native German language.

"You must turn from your ways, for the day of the Lord is at hand!" shouted the other man, staring intently at each person in the crowd.

"This is garbage," said the Prince. "They're just like all the other kooks claiming to be Christ."

At that moment, both men looked directly at the Prince, noticing him with his crowd of bodyguards.

The first one stated, "Beware Israel, the serpent seeks to destroy you. Do not be deceived."

The Prince glared back at the men without even a twitch.

The second one continued with his eyes fixed upon the Prince. "Oh Wicked one, your doom is sealed. You have but a short time before the King of Kings will set up His glorious Kingdom."

"What a joke," the Prince stated, turning back around. "These guys ought to be put into an insane asylum."

He began pushing his way through the crowd with the other bodyguards. I followed close behind him, helping the Prime Minister's efforts to keep up.

"These type of idiots give us a bad name," the Prime Minister said in a disgusted voice. "With all the great blessings we are receiving from God, how can anyone talk about our needing to repent?"

After returning to the limousine, the Prince phoned one of military officers. "Yes, send down a division and kill them. I want to make an example of these two. This type of preaching could hurt the morale of both Israel and the Federation. Use extreme caution. What? Yes, whatever weapons are necessary. Thanks."

"Prime Minister, please make sure the press in your country doesn't receive any more leaks about these two," the Prince stated.

"You're right, but what about some of the television coverage they've already received?" the Prime Minister asked.

"That's okay, it may have worked to our advantage. I'll make some phone calls to the media presidents and we'll have them blow it off as just some more Christ impersonators. After I have them killed, it will be old news."

Jacob Rubenstein wanted to see the two prophets for himself. Many talked about the two old men as fanatical preachers dressed in old, dirty clothes as just another gimmick. However, some were saying these men were sent from the Lord to spread the news of the coming Kingdom which had been prophesied in the Scriptures. He was walking down the street back to his apartment when a crowd of people caught his eye. He turned down the street, hearing deep voices shout in his native Russian language. He pushed his way close to the front, straining on his toes to view the scene.

In his efforts to see the spectacle, Jacob failed to hear the shouts of the armed guards behind him. Without warning, he felt the strong hands grasp his shoulders and toss him to the ground. His head hit another man's shoulder causing both to fall into an elderly lady as they crashed to the ground. Blood droplets formed from the scrapes on his arms and hands. He stood back up, wondering who could have thrown him to the side so easily. The uniformed guards stood in a semi-circle around the Prince and the Prime Minister. Another guard, whom Jacob recognized from television, stood next to the Prince, dwarfing those around him.

"The arrogance of some people," Jacob muttered to himself.

"What a joke," he heard the Prince say. His bodyguards turned around and made their way back down the street while hundreds of admirers rushed to see the Prince and Prime Minister.

Jacob wanted to hear what the two men were saying, so he again made his way to the front.

"Repent! Turn back to the Living and True God of your fore-fathers. Bring forth fruits worthy of the King. He is coming soon! Prepare your hearts, O Israel. Prepare ye the way of the Lord!" one of the men shouted.

The other man continued, "the God of Abraham, Isaac and Jacob, the God of our fathers, has glorified His Son, Jesus, who was delivered up, and denied in the presence of Pilate, when he was determined to let Him go. But, they denied the Holy One and the Just, and desired a murderer to be granted unto them; and killed the Prince of Life, whom God has raised from the dead, whereof we are witnesses. Repent ye therefore and be converted, that your sins may be blotted out, when the times of refreshing shall come from the presence of the Lord. Unto you, God, having raised up His Son, Jesus, sent Him to bless you, in turning everyone of you from his iniquities."

At this, many of the ones listening turned and walked away, shaking their heads. Still, others continued to move into the spots vacated, to hear the two start over again. Jacob slid his way into the front row along with other curious spectators.

On the other side of the street, a group of Federation soldiers lined up with guns in ready position. The Federation Captain proudly strutted out to the two preachers with ten soldiers marching right behind.

"Under authority of the Federation, you must be executed for your crimes against world peace," the captain shouted for all to hear. "Ready, aim...."

The two elderly men opened their mouths as if to speak, when a trail of fire shot out towards their aggressors. The ball of fire engulfed the soldiers with a bright orange blaze. Within seconds, the charred remains lay smoldering in the street. The two preachers continued after a moment of silence, as if unaffected by the ordeal. Much of the crowd, stunned during the brief fight, began running in fear. Jacob turned and ran with them, not stopping until he was safely inside his home, shutting the door behind him. How could anyone understand what was going on in this changing world, he thought to himself.

Day 840

"You heard me. Stop all their transactions immediately," the Prince stated in a sharp tone. "England, Belgium and the Netherlands have no place in the World Currency Exchange as of right now. Take care of it immediately!"

"We'll see how long it takes before we get results," the Prince spoke in disgusted tones to the Austrian president. "No one will mess with my decisions anymore. It is time for the world to see who the next leader will be."

"How long do you think it will take?" the Austrian president asked.

"We'll hear from them this evening, as soon as they realize they have no way to trade with other countries," the Prince replied with a smile.

I wondered if the problems could be solved as quickly as the Prince said. The three Presidents of England, Belgium and the Netherlands had opposed the Prince to his face in front of several dignitaries. They did not want to enforce the World Church as the official religion for their countries. They also did not like their share of Babylon, feeling the Prince had given too much to Austria and himself.

"The Pope wishes to speak to you," the intercom blared.

"Thank you. Hello," the Prince stated in his cheerful voice. "I have just shut them off of the World Currency Exchange system. I should hear from them in a couple hours. Yes, once we get this settled it will pave the way to the executions without opposition. I

44

would like to get rid of those who oppose our one world religion, but we must do it in a more delicate manner. Two months of preparation will help the process dramatically. Yes, I just talked to the President of the United States. With your continuous support the law should get through Congress this week. Yes, Yes. No, it shouldn't be a problem. We covered up the deaths of the soldiers as well. Of course, people will always talk about it, but the media followed our orders and just casually mentioned the outbreak of even more crazy Christ impersonators. There's nothing more I can do. They've killed everyone we've sent, even the snipers from three blocks away. No, I don't think so. The Prime Minister warns people of the destructive attitude of these two toward Israel, and how they threaten to ruin everything Israel has gained. Yes. Yes. With my continued support, and revealing of my Jewish ancestry to the Prime Minister, I'd say in six months Israel will be mine!"

Sveta Rubenstein set the food on the table for her family. Her husband, Jacob, quickly grabbed the plate of meat while, her three kids fought for the vegetables and fruit. She was thankful for the extra food their family had from their garden out in the country. Even Jerusalem felt the shortage of food in the world evidenced by the high prices at the market. She often thought about what it would be like if they hadn't left Russia several years ago to migrate back to their rebuilt homeland. God had been very good to their family.

"Did you hear what happened today?" Jacob asked her.

"No, I haven't had a chance to listen to the news," she replied.

"The Prince appointed three new Presidents for England, Belgium and the Netherlands. With the United States adopting the World Church yesterday, that means we are the only country in the world not a part of the World religion. They also announced the executions to begin as scheduled in less then 2 months!"

"What about us?" asked Timothy, the sixteen year old, eldest son. "Will we have to conform?"

"I don't know, son, the Prince has been very kind to our country since the very beginning. Many say he is a Jew. I just don't think he could really control us enough to break off the sacrifice and our ancient religion."

"How come we don't observe all the traditions of our religion?" Natasha, the fifteen year old daughter asked.

"When we left Russia, I told you we wanted to be in our homeland. I think God has done many things for our people, but many Jews don't believe in religion. Remember all the conflicts about the sacrifices before they started?"

"But Dad," thirteen year old and youngest son Paul argued, "don't you think it was God who saved our country from the Russians?"

"Yes, son, that's why we have gone to the synagogue a few times, just to see what it was like. But ever since I saw the two prophets, I just don't know what to think."

"Is that why you have been reading that Russian Bible you were given when we were still in Russia?" Natasha asked.

"Yes, I've been reading the Bible from the beginning and I want to read it all."

"What does it say, Dad?" Paul questioned, still chewing the food in his mouth.

"Well, it talks about how Israel started and came out of Egypt according to the first few books in the Bible. Then I've read about our history, how God always blessed us when we followed Him, but our ancestors always turned away and God punished them for it. Yet, He always brought us back to the land He promised us. I've just been reading the prophets, and they keep mentioning that God Himself will come from our nation and rule the world from here in Jerusalem."

"Wow, do you think it will happen?" Paul asked.

"I'm not sure yet. But, it amazes me how our nation could come back after almost nineteen hundred years of oblivion," the father replied, shaking his head as in unbelief.

Day 910

"One hundred thousand a day? Good. Keep up the pace. The sooner we rid ourselves of these menaces, the sooner we move to unite the world's spiritual focus. All people who preach about Jesus Christ's coming kingdom must be exterminated....All!" the Prince commanded then hung up the phone.

"How is the ship movement in the Mediterranean going General?" the Prince said to President Carlos.

"We have increased our reserves by a total of five more ships, two within twenty miles of Israel's coast," President Carlos explained.

"Okay, that should be enough for now. I don't want to alarm Israel or any other country. We will wait to see what happens with Russia's troop movement," the Prince said with a nod of approval.

As the Prince and President Carlos began scrutinizing maps of the Middle East, I turned to gaze upon the buildings of scenic Madrid from our limousine. This would be the final stop of our Federation tour of Spiritual Centers.

We parked in front of a magnificent stone cathedral on the Northern outskirts of Madrid. The Prince's surprise visits acquainted him with the mood and response of the individual centers. As always, the beggars could be seen in the surrounding areas of the Spiritual Center, hoping for a morsel of food. By law, they are not permitted within 500 feet of any religious edifice, to assure the safety and comfort of those attending, punishable by immediate execution.

The Prince led the way up the stairs and through the glass doors, bypassing the stunned prostitutes who were sitting around the entrance. The custom of many of the incorporated religions is to engage in sexual relations with women while offering incense and money to the spiritual forces of earth. The Prince never took part in this behavior, choosing instead to present some sort of gift at an altar and listen to one of the many services. We took a seat as a priest in a white robe took his place at the podium, beginning his message about peace with ourselves and with God. Many of the Spiritual Centers are converted from old church buildings, while others are modern architectural structures. The sunlight sparkled through three colorful tinted windows, illuminating the rejuvenated interior of the ancient chapel. After the sermon, the Prince handed the priest a golden statue, studded with diamonds and emeralds.

For the past couple of months, the Rubenstein family had gathered every evening to read and study their Russian Bible. After a portion of the Scriptures was read aloud, everyone would voice their thoughts and questions about the passage. If a question was raised, to which no one could offer an acceptable answer, Jacob would search out a possible solution and present the information at the next reading.

"In that day, shall there be upon the bells of the horses, holiness unto the Lord; and the pots in the Lord's house shall be like the bowls before the altar. Yea, every pot in Jerusalem and in Judah shall be holiness unto the Lord of Hosts; and all they that sacrifice shall come and take of them, and seethe therein; and in that day there shall be no more the Canaanite in the house of the Lord of Hosts." Jacob sat back in the old blanket-covered recliner. "That concludes the book of Zechariah."

"That was really weird, Dad," Paul exclaimed.

"I didn't understand most of it," Timothy stated.

"What I find odd, is how our King will be human enough to ride a donkey," Sveta pointed out, "but, He is still going to come down to the Mount of Olives and split it into two parts.

How can both happen?"

"Is our King supposed to be called the Branch and actually grow up among our people?" Paul asked.

"What about those thirty pieces of silver? How can God be priced at only thirty pieces of silver?" Sveta questioned, shaking her head.

After a few moments of silence, Jacob said, "I think it is interesting that the end of Zechariah is like a fairy tale, that God will make everything right again. Every nation that has hurt our people will be punished with a plague and our King will reign over the entire earth."

"That plague is cool," Timothy interrupted.

"What do you mean?" Jacob asked.

"It says that the eyes, tongue and skin will actually melt off while the people and animals are standing on their feet! Kind of like one of those horror movies, but in real life!"

"Jacob!" Sveta gasped, her eyes opened in amazement. "That's exactly what happens when a hydrogen bomb explodes! God already knew how to do it almost three thousand years ago. Maybe man's invention is a fulfillment of God's prophecy."

"I never thought about it that way." Jacob replied. "I wonder how many of these prophecies are already fulfilled and which ones are still in the future. Like this one about...let's see if I can find it."

Jacob looked forward turning back the pages and glancing down the rows of words with his finger. "Here it is, chapter twelve, verse ten, *And I will pour upon the house of David and upon the inhabitants of Jerusalem, the Spirit of Grace and of supplications: and they shall look upon Me whom they have pierced, and they shall mourn for Him, as one mourneth for his only son, and shall be in bitterness for him, as one that is in bitterness for his firstborn.*"

"It's almost like there are two different Kings for us," Sveta interjected. "How can we mourn for someone who is wounded and still be excited about His triumphant victory for Israel? It doesn't make sense."

"Wait a second!" Jacob said. "I remember that another passage in Isaiah said the same thing."

He quickly turned in his Bible while the family waited quietly. "Here it is underlined in chapter fifty-three, verse five, *But He was wounded for our transgressions, He was bruised for our iniquities: the chastisement of our peace was upon Him, and with His stripes we are healed.* Verse four says, *Surely he hath borne our griefs, and carried our sorrows: yet we did esteem Him stricken, smitten of God, and afflicted.*"

Jacob sat back in his chair, rubbing his hand to his forehead in disbelief. "I remember how this didn't make sense to me before. Maybe we have two Kings."

"What if it's just not true?" Natasha questioned. "What if this is all garbage and we're wasting our time?"

"But what about us coming from Russia along with millions of other Jews from around the world?" Timothy asked in an arrogant voice. "We keep reading these prophecies about Israel coming back and here we are after nineteen hundred years just like God has promised."

"That's true," Jacob replied nodding his head. "Even in Zechariah it keeps talking about the day of Israel's return and none of this was possible until now."

"I don't like how God will turn upon children," Paul exclaimed.

"God doesn't say that. I don't think." Sveta answered.

"The Bible said He would turn against little ones," Paul asserted. "Since I'm thirteen, I'm not considered little anymore, am I?"

"Oh honey, I'm sure you'll be okay. It doesn't mean you." Sveta reassured.

"Here it is," Jacob stated. "*Awake, O sword, against my shepherd, and against the man that is my fellow, saith the Lord of Hosts: smite the Shepherd, and the sheep shall be scattered: and I will turn mine hand upon the little ones. And it shall come to pass that in all the land, saith the Lord, two parts therein shall be cut off and die; but the third shall be left there-in.* That's interesting. It says that two-thirds of the people will die and only one-third will live."

"But that's not for us, is it dear?" Sveta asked hopefully.

"I guess it depends on if it already is in history or if it is a part of this future prophecy. Hey wait, this may be the answer in verse nine: *And I will bring the third part through the fire, and will refine them as silver is refined, and will try them as gold is tried; they shall call on my name, and I will hear them; I will say, it is My people; and they shall say, the Lord is my God.*"

"How is that the answer, Dad?" Timothy questioned.

"Well, it seems that only one third of the people will make it through a testing time and be able to proclaim God as Lord. We haven't come to that point yet," Jacob answered.

"You mean two-thirds of everyone in Israel now — will die?" Sveta asked with disbelief in her voice.

Jacob looked at his family with tears in his eyes. "Only if the Bible is true."

Day 1080

"An earthquake?" the Prince exclaimed with surprise. "How big was it? I see, what other damage? How badly was Babylon damaged? That's good news. Get all the information and call me."

He hung up the air phone and handed it back to the secretary.

"Well, Joseph, it seems we just missed the biggest earthquake in the world."

"What happened?" I anxiously asked, thankful that we were in flight from Babylon to Jerusalem.

"An earthquake measuring seven on the Richter scale just erupted over the world." he answered.

"You mean it was a seven everywhere?" I asked.

"So far, the reports are confirming it."

The secretary stepped up. "Excuse me sir, the Pope is on the phone."

"Thank you," the Prince acknowledged. "Hello. I've already heard. Good, glad to hear everyone is all right. Yes, we will inform the media heads to show the destruction in America and the other countries first and foremost. What a shame, but that tower was going to fall sooner or later. Hey, that's a good angle. Show the destruction of the Federation as buildings that were out of date and going to fall anyway. Yes, Good. No, Russia and Egypt continue to cause dissension. The Russian President threatened to withdraw from the currency and possibly use force against some other nations. Of course, that's why I'm on my way to Tel Aviv. President Carlos and

I are working on defensive measures for Israel and are preparing for the worst. He should call anytime. Yes, most of the kingdom preachers were removed. There seem to be reports out of Israel of Jewish proclaimers traveling throughout Israel. They may be converts from those two miserable, old fools. Not yet, but our time will come. Okay, I have another call. I'll call you after the meetings in Tel Aviv. Thanks. Bye."

"President Carlos on line two, sir."

"Thank you," he answered, flashing a smile to his secretary. "Hello, President. Is everyone okay? That's great news. No, we were already in flight from Babylon. What else has happened? They need to get all their ships out of there. Go ahead and call the President of the United States to warn him that we don't want any American casualties. He will need to pull out all ships from the Mediterranean Sea. What is our total ship count there? I'm going to propose we bring in thirty total. If we can that would seal up our control of the Middle East. No. No. I'd say twenty ships in the Persian Gulf should do it. Do we really have any more to spare? I didn't think so. What is the current status of troops on the Eastern front? Uh huh, good. I don't think we will need them, but I want to have them ready. If the Russians won't back down, we may have to take action."

The Rubenstein family stepped off the bus and began walking down the dirt road towards their small plot of fenced land. This was the last time before winter to reap the vegetables still left in the garden and take them back to the city. With the extra food from the garden they could afford to eat three meals a day, while those of other nations struggled with the famine.

The sun's full glory could be seen between the hills as the bright blue skies chased the last of the night sky to the west. The early chill of the Autumn morning faded while the Rubenstein's walked in silence, still not fully awake.

Jacob opened the white fence door, holding it while the family marched past ready for the task at hand.

As he latched the door, Jacob stopped and looked around. Where were the birds? Where were the squirrels? Nothing moved, except for a few other families walking to their gardens. Something was amiss. The blue skies quickly disappeared as darkness settled like a blanket over the land.

"Dad!" Paul screamed. "What's going on?"

Before Jacob could answer, the ground began to move beneath his feet. Sveta screamed and dropped the bag of garden tools cradled in her arms. Natasha wrapped her arms around her mother, while Timothy and Paul dove to the feet of Jacob.

"Stay on the ground!" Jacob yelled over the increasing rumble noise.

Not able to withstand the violent shaking any longer, Jacob fell to his hands and knees. A bright flash of light illuminated his family clutching the ground. Another streak of light shot down from the sky. "This is the end," he thought to himself. "The Almighty God is going to wipe us out. No where to hide. Am I ready to face Him?"

The noise continued to grow until Jacob finally screamed out, at the top of his lungs, "Have mercy on us, O God!"

As quickly as the event began, the noise hushed into a perfect stillness. The sun's veil lifted and the stars faded back into the lightened sky. Jacob and Sveta looked up first, listening to the first chirps of a nearby finch signaling the return of safety.

"I'm scared, Dad," Paul whimpered.

"I am too, son," Jacob replied, thinking about the words he had uttered to God.

"Did God do that?" Natasha asked.

"Who else would?" Timothy snapped.

"I think it's time to ask God for the answers," Sveta said softly.

"What? Hmm, maybe we should," Jacob stated.

Sveta continued, "We have read almost the entire Scriptures and I know God is warning our people as He warned us before in the Bible."

"If there really is a God, He should answer His own chosen people if they want answers," Paul quipped.

"What about the new part in our Bible? Timothy questioned.

"We aren't supposed to read it, according to the priests," Jacob replied, "but maybe the answers are there."

After a moment of silence, Jacob began, "Okay, let's ask God to give us answers. If the Bible is true, God will heed our request."

Jacob bowed his head, shutting his eyes tightly. "God, I don't know what to say or how to say it. If You are there and we are really Your chosen people, please give us answers to what is happening."

The family continued a moment in silent prayer until Jacob opened his eyes and saw two men standing at the gate.

"Who are you?" Jacob gasped in surprise.

The rest of the family looked up to the two young men dressed in farmer's clothes. Their clean shaven faces and smiles shone with an aura of calmness that overpowered the Rubenstein's.

"We're just passing through and noticed your family praying," the curly, dark-haired one said.

"Uh, didn't you just feel the earthquake?" Jacob asked.

"Of course, another of the Lord's judgments has passed," replied the one with straight blonde hair.

How do you know that?" Jacob asked with amazement.

"The Scriptures clearly teach God's plan for our time. This is only the beginning of sorrows, the worst is yet to come," the dark-haired man replied with deadly seriousness.

"We've been reading the Bible also, but I'm still confused about our nation, the Messiah and prophecy," Jacob stated. With a pause he asked, "Can you help us?"

The two men looked at each other and smiled. "We've been sent to do just that!"

They opened the gate and sat down with the family, while some neighbors looked curiously at the gathering. Pulling Bibles out from their coats, they began teaching about Jesus.

After awhile, Jacob shook his head and said, "You mean Jesus fulfilled all these prophecies in the Scriptures? Why haven't we been taught this? Jesus is the Messiah!"

Sveta exclaimed, "I understand how He was humble and died the first time, and when He comes this next time, He will fulfill the prophecies of his kingship and our nation. But what about the events now?"

Natasha interrupted. "Yeah, what will happen to us?"

The two men sympathetically looked at each other with sighs of sadness. "Part of your answer lies within you," the blond-haired man replied.

"The other part is in Scriptures, but only God knows the outcome of your life here," the other man answered.

Anxiously, Jacob questioned, "What do you mean?"

The dark-haired man continued, "Your eternal destiny lies within your soul, as to whether you will accept Jesus' completed work on the cross for your own sins, and as to your place in His completed kingdom. To trust in Jesus will assure your eternal life and a place in the coming kingdom."

"To reject Him," the blonde-haired man added, "is to bring eternal destruction upon yourself and banishment into the Lake of Fire reserved for Satan and his angels."

"As the Scriptures foretold," the other man continued, "and your soul confirms, your sins needed a great sacrifice. Only Jesus could fulfill all the prophecies and prove His deity by His own resurrection. Jesus was the only person without sin of his own and the only one capable of love great enough to offer himself as the one sacrifice for sins which could be accepted by the Father in Heaven. Hebrews ten, verse ten states, *We are sanctified through the offering of the body of Jesus Christ once for all.* And Isaiah fifty three, verse five reads, *But He was wounded for our transgressions, He was bruised for our iniquities: the chastisement of our peace was upon him; and with His stripes we are healed."*

The dark-haired man paused for a moment, then added, "Now each of you has to decide to reject or accept Jesus as your Savior and King, thus fulfilling God's destiny for your soul."

Without hesitation, Jacob sobbed, "I believe."

The tears rolled down the sides of his face. So many emotions filled his regenerated heart: joyfulness of knowing his eternal life;

peace that melted the fear of death and uncertainty, gladness in knowing how much Jesus loved the wretched sinner that he was; sadness, in realizing that his sins sent Jesus to the cross, excitement in the truthfulness of the Scriptures.

He didn't understand why he was crying and smiling at the same time.

Each of Jacob's family cried softly and whispered, "I believe," experiencing the same emotions as Jacob.

"Praise God!" both men exclaimed.

For a few moments the members of the family clung to one another joyfully. Then Jacob looked up to the two men. "What now?"

"Now comes the most difficult part," the dark-haired man stated. "You will need to study your Scriptures more fervently than before. The answers to what will happen are contained within God's Word. The Holy Spirit will guide you in them. However, what part in the future on earth there is for each of you...only the Lord knows."

The two men stood up, smiled at the family and nodded their heads in approval. As they turned to leave, Jacob reached out with his hand and said, "wait."

Without stopping, the two men shut the gate behind them. The blonde-haired man turned his head with a smile. "Don't be anxious, the Holy Spirit will guide you."

"You are not alone," the two men echoed as they walked down the road and out of sight.

Day 1122

The plane dropped below the clouds, revealing the old ten story apartment buildings on the Northern outskirts of Moscow. The once mighty empire, now reeling under the power-hungry dictator, was like a bear robbed of it's cubs. After the fall of communism and it's devastating defeat at the hands of Israel, Russia again was flexing it's muscles in the Middle East with military build up, hoping to regain pride and food for the starving. Egypt, backed up by the Palestinian Liberation Organization (PLO) was again allying with Russia in hopes of expelling the Jews from their claimed land. The Prince's visit with the Russian President could mean peace, or another world war.

"Yes, just as planned, we now have a full supplement of ships in the Persian Gulf and off the coast of Israel. We have sent two more divisions in efforts to reduce the likelihood of attack. No, I've sent them to Jerusalem to the new headquarters. We are slowly fortifying our military presence in Israel. If the Russians won't listen, I'll force them to listen. Okay. I'll call you then. Be ready for the momentary shutdown if needed. Nothing will stop the New World Order!"

The Prince stepped off the plane, following behind me, and surrounded by an entourage of guards. We were met by limousines whisking us away to the Kremlin. Every block was full of detailed, large stone buildings lacking in repair and attention. The streets were filled with drunks, beggars and vendors. As we pulled through the gate, the manicured lawn and bright walls of the Kremlin contrasted with the rest of the city.

Coming into the headquarters of the former "Evil Empire" as the American President Ronald Reagan once termed it, would intimidate anyone. However, being in the presence of the Prince and leading his protective guard, I feared no one. We are the elite power in the world, and I knew it.

As the Prince and the Russian Dictator exchanged greetings, I examined the room and his Russian guard. Our new designer suits, bulging with our large frames, contrasted with their dull, slightly worn military suits. The Prince, meticulously dressed, did not smile as was his usual custom, in shaking the hand of the heavy set and rougher looking Russian President. We outclassed our adversaries in weapons, dress and manners, but they portrayed a deep roughness from years of just surviving their system. We couldn't under estimate their instincts of aggression shown in the past.

The Prince's assistants brought out papers and maps which they laid out in front of the Russian President. The Prince showed the steps to shutdown their country economically and promised a full military fight to defend Israel before they would even get close to attacking. He also pointed out the Federation's control of Egypt's funds and total economic system. The Prince emphasized his peaceful intention, with no military actions necessary to work towards total world unification.

Completing the full day of talks, we drove back to the airport.

"He should respond after we talk with Egypt," the Prince stated confidently.

"Sveta!" Jacob shouted from the living room. "Russia is withdrawing it's troops from the borders!"

"Wow, are they joining with the Federation?" she asked.

"Doesn't look like it, but it may happen later," he replied.

"Does the Bible say anything about that, Dad?" Paul asked.

"I'm not sure if it does or not," Jacob answered with a puzzled frown.

"C'mon Dad, let's start before supper on our studies," Tim begged.

"Too late, dear, supper is ready," Sveta interrupted.

The dinner was served while the family discussed the news of the Prince's latest victory in coercing Egypt to pledge allegiance to world peace. Russia followed suit by removing the heavy military strongholds at their southern most borders, but not giving in to the Federation's global peace program.

As they concluded eating, Tim immediately began pushing his father to begin their nightly Scripture reading. With their new found faith in Jesus Christ as their Messiah, the New Testament became a living book for the family. They took turns reading and sharing what thoughts impressed them most. They all rushed to clear the table and bring their notes from their personal Bible readings.

Sitting in his favorite chair, Jacob set his tea cup down. "Before we begin the reading, who has something to share from their own studies?"

Without hesitation, Tim responded, "I skipped ahead to the book of Revelation. Dad, it's talking about exactly what is going on now!"

"No way, are you sure?" Paul asked.

"Yeah. I read in chapter six and it talked about the famine, earthquake, death and everything," Tim answered.

"Okay, here it is. Let me start with verse one in chapter six," Jacob stated. He read the chapter without a sound from within the room, as each intently listened to God's judgments. *"...for the great day of His wrath is come; and who shall be able to stand?"* Jacob sat stunned, looking blankly at the chapter he had just finished.

"That's exactly what has happened so far!" Sveta exclaimed.

"It even described the earthquake that brought us to the Lord," Natasha added.

"Well, it's nothing like what else is written in there. It gets a lot worse," Tim said.

Day 1250

The Prince paced back and forth across the thick, Asian carpet of his seventieth story office in Babylon. His words into the phone were harsh and full of power. His nostrils would flare occasionally as he took deep breaths to bark more commands to the Spanish General.

"No mercy! I want them crushed. Send them over the borders as soon as possible. Of course not, a nuclear war is useless. I want the land!"

The Prince calmly handed the receiver to his secretary with a smile and nod.

"Joseph, it's going to get very complicated in the next few weeks," he spoke to me in a caring way. "You will have to do exactly as I say without question."

"Yes sir. You know I will," I replied.

Before he could continue, the secretary interrupted. "It's the General on the red line."

"Hello, General. Yes. Ha! I knew they would come crawling back to us. Prepare the special troops for our little surprise to our ignorant foes. Our time has finally come!"

The Bible slid through Jacob's fingers landing on the floor with a thud.

61

"What does it mean, huh?" Sveta asked. "Are the ten kings the same as the Federation Presidents?"

Jacob shook his head slowly, staring at the red, hard cover Bible lying on the floor. With quivering lips. he stammered. "It's the Prince...he's the betrayer...he's the one who will bring the abomination...it all makes sense now."

"How, honey?" Sveta asked softly.

"I was such a fool!" Jacob responded as he quickly grabbed up the Bible, turning back the pages to Revelation. "It's right here in verse twelve of chapter seventeen. The ten kings are the same as the ten horns. The beast is the same as the fierce king in Daniel. The Federation and the Prince are these people. They are the ones who will oppose Jesus Christ and His future kingdom!"

Russia, China and India had continued to voice major concerns about the Federation and the Prince. Thousands died from starvation every day, and they blamed the Prince's programs for their economic woes. We received reports that the three countries were talking of an alliance to once again invade Israel and seize more land. The Prince, tiring of continued negotiations, ordered Federation Troops to secure positions for attack across the borders of the opposing countries. He also sent in extra military support to Israel for their defense.

General Carlos sent word to the opposing leaders that the Federation would invade immediately unless they would agree to terms of total peace. The Federation Air Force was in the air when the Russian President called to request another meeting.

The Prince's personal jet and five other planes landed in Moscow, but the Prince waited in another jet in Brussels. Instead, the six planes were loaded with heavy military and nuclear devices and hundreds of top combat soldiers. If all went as the Prince planned, the Federation could take over the three countries in a matter of hours, with very few casualties.

"That's right. I want you to order your troops to lay down their weapons. Yes. Yes, you have heard correctly. We will blow Moscow into the air in seconds, if you do not completely surrender. As I have promised, you will still be the Russian leader, but you will report to me. No, there is no alternative...you will die," the Prince calmly stated. "Good, after my field Generals call, I will talk to you again."

The Prince handed the phone back to his secretary as he grabbed the red line phone. "Yes, General. Good. On my command, we will invade the Russian borders. Stay on the line."

The secretary handed him the phone headset back. "Sir, India is on line one now."

The Prince ordered the President of India and the Dictator of China to surrender in similar fashion as the Russians. They agreed to his terms and relinquished control to the Prince.

The Prince laid down his headset and picked up the red line phone.

"Okay, sir, the field General is on the line," the secretary remarked.

"Thank you. Yes? Excellent, tell the Russians we won't shoot if they surrender their weapons, then secure the streets. Right. One thousand more troops are landing every half hour. Be gentle in dealing with the Russians, I want to avoid any fighting if possible. Good."

The Prince nodded to the secretary and she switched the line to General Carlos.

"Okay, General. Invade the borders as planned."

Jacob sat forward in his chair, his hands folded together. Concern spread over his face as he slowly looked upon each family member. "I don't know what will happen, but I think we should prepare to flee Israel."

"But why, Dad?" Natasha asked.

"According to Matthew twenty four, Jesus said that the sacrifices will be stopped, and that our people will be slaughtered like in World War II."

"You mean the Prince is going to do it?" Timothy asked in amazement.

"Yes, son, if the Scriptures are accurate, and I'm sure they are."

"But he is a friend to our people," Timothy opposed. "He's been fighting for us. The priests, the media and our President speak so highly of him."

"What about the treaty? His World Peace Plan?" Paul questioned.

"The Bible says he's lying," Jacob rebutted.

Our plane landed in Moscow with specialized armed forces cautiously unloading. The Prince followed close behind until he could see our troops lined up for him.

We boarded the bullet-proof military truck, which had been transported from the Federation for the take-over, and drove to the back entrance of the Kremlin. Federation troops opened the gate and lined our way to the inner chambers where we had walked before. This time, the Prince strolled slowly, smiling and admiring the ancient architecture.

The Russian President stood nervously awaiting the Prince's arrival. As the Prince entered, the Russian President bowed his head slowly and said sheepishly, "the country is at your disposal, Prince."

With immediate determination, the Prince replied, "The Kremlin is mine, you work for me. My troops are staying and will guard you at all times. You will be protected...as long as you obey my orders."

The Prince explained how the Russian President should handle the whole situation and even left one of his top economic advisors to help the war-torn country recover. We drove back to his personal jet and took off for Babylon.

"The Pope is on the phone, sir."

"Thank you. Hello. Everything has gone as planned. I will make the World peace speech tomorrow. Yes, I will visit both India and China afterwards. They are all under my control. Only Israel is left, but that will soon change."

Day 1251

The three familiar robed men stepped off the elevator and into the Prince's seventieth story office in Babylon. Behind them, the Austrian President and the Pope quietly talked to each other.

"Joseph, it is time for you to understand," the Prince smiled at me. "Come with us."

"I...I'm not sure...if I'm ready," I stammered with a nervousness previously unknown.

The Austrian President smiled and nodded with approval. I followed behind as we entered into the inner chambers of the Prince's office.

The room was filled with hundreds of lit candles around the room. Five candles burned at the corners of the encircled star, painted in the middle of the floor. The three priests immediately kneeled around the circle, bowing their heads in prayer. The Prince escorted me behind one of the priests, and we knelt down. My heart raced with anticipation and fear. My hands shook without control. I was afraid. No man on earth could ever make me tremble, but I knew this was not natural. The tension prevented me from swallowing. My mouth was drying from the quickened breaths.

After a few minutes, which seemed like hours, one of the priests began to utter strange, unearthly sounds. He let out an ear-piercing scream and doubled over to the floor. The two other priests also screamed and bowed to the floor. They raised up, the hoods falling off their heads, revealing their old and wrinkled baldness. The candlelight danced in their totally black eyes. I shuttered throughout my body from their hellish presence.

In the same low voice I'd heard before, the priest's lips moved slowly. "The time has come. The world is ready for our Master and Lord. He shuns the presence of the enemy. Lucifer wants his throne on earth. Are you ready Chosen One to receive the power?"

"I am ready," the Prince replied confidently.

The priest turned slowly to the Pope, and the unearthly voice continued, "...the time is now at hand for the worker to complete the perfect trinity. Are you ready for the power?"

"I am ready," the Pope replied.

"Good," the voice answered with a deep, sinister laugh. "The world awaits their king. There is only one mission to accomplish for the world to be ours forever!"

"Who is this new one?" Another deep but cracking voice asked.

"He is my servant," the Prince replied.

"Oh king of Persia," the other voice continued. "May we take him?"

"Do as you wish, but the time is short," the first voice answered.

I took a deep, gasping breath. They were talking about me. I had never been taught to run, and where could I go?

Before I could think, I felt a presence invade my being. I started choking, coughing. Pain shot through my whole body. My head wanted to explode. I felt violated. I was not my own. I had no control. My hands were grabbing my own gun. I was falling into a chasm. The gun was pointing at me. I could hear a voice echo outside. "Don't kill him, the Master will use him."

I'm falling deeper into the pit. The light is fading away. The noises are disappearing. The pain, the pain.

Jacob hastened home, not wanting to miss the Prince's world peace speech. He bounded up the steps and unlocked the apartment door.

"It's just starting!" Sveta exclaimed.

"The world is in a state of peace," the Prince broadcast. "No blood will be shed by the leaders of Russia, China or India. We obtained our goal of worldwide peace, thanks to the combined efforts of all involved. The Federation will continue controlling Russia, China and India until we feel they can co-exist with us in total peace. Because of this great day in the history of our planet, I am declaring tomorrow as a World Peace Holiday!"

The crowd cheered wildly for several minutes. The TV commentators ecstatically acclaimed the Prince's victory.

The Prince continued, "we now have a New World Order. One that controls peace and prosperity. It is time for us to reach our full potential. Follow me into utopia! Follow me in this coming New Age."

"At least I understand how this is against God," Sveta remarked.

"Right," Jacob replied. "But I'm still not sure when our problems begin. I know it's going to be soon, but when?"

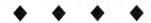

I woke up lying on the couch in the Prince's office with a severe headache. He was behind his desk working on papers as usual.

"How are you feeling?" the Prince asked.

"Umm, fine, except for a headache," I replied.

"Rest up, because much work is to be done."

"Yes sir," I replied, drinking from a glass of water left next to the couch. What had happened? I began trembling from the thoughts of the night before. It was the most terrifying experience in my life. Did I still want to stay involved? Did I have a choice? Who is this King of Persia and Lucifer? I closed my eyes and fell back to sleep.

Later in the afternoon, I was up and walking around, checking on security reports, when the Prince called me to his desk.

"You must listen carefully," he warned. "It is important that you follow my instructions precisely."

"Yes, sir," I replied.

"Good. In a few days we will be traveling to the Vatican. You will come, but you will not be near me during my speech to the people. You will wait at the appointed place. While I'm on the podium, one of my enemies will put a dagger in my back."

"What?" I exclaimed. "But..."

"Listen now, Joseph. This is where you will help me. As the ambulance arrives, you will give me a drug that will stop my heart and brain activity. It will make me look completely lifeless. However, the bleeding from my wound will cease and allow my body to recover. From the point that you give this to me, until I come to, you must not leave my side or allow anything to touch my body. Do you understand this?"

"Yes sir," I replied.

"Good. The Austrian President will make sure that you have control. Do whatever is necessary to preserve my body. Now, here's a detailed list that..."

Day 1258

I felt odd not guarding the Prince as he stood behind the podium in front of the Vatican. Normally, I would watch for any sign of danger regarding his life, but now I must quench my normal instincts and allow the consequences to happen. The thought of the Palatial guards failing miserably, brought some satisfaction to my otherwise distraught soul. As I watched the Prince speak from a distance for the first time, I began wondering who he really is. This amazing man who now controls the world, can be so kind and gentle, but forceful if needed. I've seen his viciousness in wanting world power, yet smoothness with negotiations. He possesses raw power in economic policy, followed by persistence for worldwide prosperity. More important, who or what controls him?

As my imaginations swirled with the many thoughts, I noticed someone dressed in church clothing approach the podium. The sunlight flashed off the shiny metal blade he withdrew from his robe. The Palatial guards reacted too late as the man grabbed the Prince's right shoulder, immediately thrusting the dagger deep into his back. I stepped forward with a whimper watching my Prince crumble to the ground without a sound. His orders echoed loudly in my head as I so much wanted to help, but knew I shouldn't. His obvious control, even of his own death, held my feet to the ground next to the ambulance.

The whole entourage of medical and security personnel rushed toward me pushing the Prince's bed with his life-support systems already attached. The media could not pass the police barricade, but continued to move into positions for filming. I could hear the crowd's hysteria, and wondered if anyone might get hurt from possible ensuing riots. Everyone was barking out orders to each other as the Prince's body rolled up to the ambulance.

"Doctor Kernstein and myself will be the only two accompanying the Prince to the hospital," I stated loudly for all to hear.

"Who on earth are you?" The emergency doctor questioned.

"I'm going with him, period," the top Palatial guard stated.

Doctor Kernstein, the Prince's personal physician, began setting up the medical equipment as the bed was loaded into the ambulance. I put up my arms preventing both men from proceeding further.

"Get out of my way," snarled the guard.

"Let me pass, young man," the emergency doctor snapped.

"I am Joseph Van Buren, Captain of the Prince's sentinel, with explicit orders for an emergency. His doctor and I travel alone."

"Well, I'm in charge here!" the emergency doctor shouted.

"Not any more," I stated as I picked the scrawny man up off the ground and tossed him back into the crowd of medical officers.

"Hey! You're on our area and I have orders to watch over the Prince everywhere." The guard stated.

"I think you've done enough already," I said, immediately thrusting my clenched fist into his forehead between the eyebrows. His legs collapsed from under him and he sprawled to the ground in a heap. "Lieutenant, make sure we are surrounded by our guards as we go to the hospital, and not these idiotic fools."

"Yes, sir," The Prince's officer acknowledged. I jumped into the back of the ambulance and shut the doors as we started to the hospital.

"Are you ready to proceed as ordered?" I questioned the doctor.

"Yes, sir," he replied.

"You may begin." I said, looking at my watch.

The doctor injected the drug into the Prince's vein. The small gasps of breath ceased. His body became motionless.

"I hope the Prince knows what he is doing," I stated.

"What do you think now, Jacob?" Sveta asked. "The Prince is dead."

Jacob continued to stare at the television newscast. He shook his head in disbelief. "I don't know, honey. I just don't know."

"Dad, does this mean we'll be safe now?" Paul asked.

"No," Jacob stated as if coming out of a trance. "The Bible is clear that we will have a rough time before the Lord Jesus returns. We must stay prepared to leave on a moments notice. Is that understood?"

"I guess so," Paul answered nonchalantly.

"But Dad, you have to be wrong." Natasha interrupted. "You said the Prince was the anti-Christ. He can't be now."

"Does this mean the Bible's wrong?" Timothy questioned.

"Listen," Jacob said, "We know the Bible is true and God is not wrong. Maybe I missed something and it will be someone else. But my mistakes in guessing who it might be do not change the facts of Scripture. It says in Matthew 24 that someone will desecrate the temple and we are to flee into the mountains when it happens. We are not to come back to our apartment for anything. Does everyone understand this?"

"Yes," chorused the family.

"Where will we go?" Natasha asked.

"I think we will head to an old ancient city in Jordan."

"Jordan?" Sveta asked in amazement. "Why there?"

"Because I think there is a place that can hold millions of us Jews. It's always been known as a refuge," Jacob replied.

"What's it's name. Dad?" Timothy asked.

"It's known as the city of Petra."

Day 1260

 The past 2 days of watching over the Prince's lifeless body proved to be the limit of my patience. The short cat naps, always being interrupted by some commotion, have not been sufficient for restoring the lack of rest. After his pronounced death, hundreds, maybe thousands of reporters and so called friends have unsuccessfully attempted to see him. Then this morning, the morticians prepared the Prince's burial while I made sure that no drugs or embalming fluids came in contact with him. As they finally laid him in the coffin and closed the lid with thousands of pictures being taken, I felt a burden lifted from my shoulders as my orders had been carried out.

 I checked the coffin lid to make sure it was locked, and I took my place in the Jeep behind the decorated trailer carrying the Prince. Unlike the other mourning people, I waited with anticipation to what would transpire. I know the Prince predicted he would heal, and the drug he took would wear off, but when? If it didn't happen before he was laid in the tomb, what would I do then?

 The processional passed through the streets of Rome for almost two hours. I watched the millions of admirers paying their last respects to the Prince. Television cameras flanked our cars and perched on just about every building we passed. President Carlos ordered all networks from every country to air the funeral, but I don't think it mattered. This event was too big to miss.

The vehicles drove up to St. Peters church and began their entrance through the gates. I was closely watching for any sign when the latches unlocked and fell open. I grabbed the dash of the Jeep. Suddenly the Prince's arm thrust the coffin lid to the side! He sat up and gazed about. Our Jeep screeched to a halt. I wanted to jump out but something held me in my place.

The Prince stood up and yelled, "I'm alive! I'm back from the dead!"

He threw off his suit coat and fastened his hand on his buttoned shirt. Tearing the shirt off his muscular body, he exposed the healed knife wound on his back.

Nothing could hold me back now, I jumped out of the Jeep and ran to the Prince. Bowing down on one knee, I shouted, "Hail to the Prince!"

Other guards and policemen joined me on the ground, chorusing my chant to the Prince. The spectators who had been cheering, began shouting "Hail to the Prince!"

I looked up to his face as he glowed with abundant energy from within being fed by millions of worshipers. He wasn't just the leader of Europe, he was the King of the earth!

The Rubenstein family sat in silence watching the Prince pronounce his victory over death. Jacob stood up and walked into the kitchen. Sveta followed close behind. "What's the matter, Jacob?" She asked.

"I don't know what to think anymore," he replied. "I'm just totally confused with everything."

"God will show us what to do. He's in control and nothing is a surprise to Him," she reassured.

"I'm glad your faith is so strong. It is really good to know I'm not alone," Jacob stated looking at her.

"Of course not, dear. I love you." Sveta leaned up and kissed him on the cheek. "Hey, why don't we go to the park in the center and take some food for a family picnic. It's a nice spring day and we have a long week ahead of us."

"That sounds good. Let's see if the kids want to go." Jacob replied.

Paul and Natasha readily agreed and helped pack their meager dinner. Timothy wanted to work on his computer and finish some homework. He waved out his window as the family walked to the bus stop.

"Are the troops ready?" The Prince asked President Carlos.

"Yes, sir. All men are waiting for the signal," the President replied.

"Excuse me sir, it's the Pope," the Prince's secretary interrupted.

"Yes," the Prince answered. "Good. Plan on joining me in a few days. Our time is now here. We're landing right now."

"Joseph," the Prince snapped, "no one is to touch me, is that understood? No one."

"Yes, sir," I replied, taken aback by his rough manner.

The plane landed and we stepped out to a roaring ovation by thousands of Jews. Nine other planes loaded with Federation troops unloaded into military vehicles.

The Prince picked up his red-line phone as the procession of vehicles passed through Jerusalem. "Are the ships in position? Good. As soon as your vehicles are at the Israeli headquarters I'll call the Prime Minister."

One half of our procession broke off towards the Israeli headquarters while the Prince's entourage continued toward old Jerusalem. I sat back in my seat next to the Prince. I wasn't even nervous about our takeover of Israel. I knew he had control of the whole situation. However, his fiery eyes and the sharp tone of his voice caused me to wonder who was in control of the Prince.

The limousine stopped in front of the new Jewish temple. We waited for a few minutes until President Carlos called on the red-line phone.

"Yes," the Prince answered. "Good, I'll call now. Begin the plan."

The Prince nodded to his secretary as she said, "It's going through now."

"Hello, Prime Minister," the Prince said in his calm, cool voice. "No, we are not out front. We are by the temple. Right now, our soldiers are entering your building with President Carlos. Our ships are in the Mediterranean with guns and missiles pointed at targets throughout Israel and our air force is in the air ready to attack. What do I want?" The Prince began laughing. "First, signal your men to lay down their guns immediately or you will be shot by five different marksmen already in the building. If you make any sudden movements or lay down the phone they will shoot. Is it done? Good. Now signal President Carlos over to you. He's coming. Good. Follow his explicit instructions or you and all your country will die. The treaty? Treaties are for fools! Consider the treaty terminated and your country--mine!"

The Prince hung up the phone laughing. He nodded to a commander. Soldiers rushed into the outer court and through the surrounding area. After the Israeli soldiers surrendered their guns, I stepped out, with the Prince following behind. He confidently walked ahead to the curtains in front of the Holiest of Holies in the temple. The Priests shouted at the Prince, warning him of God's judgments upon anyone entering the sacred place. The Prince stopped in front of the curtains and turned around facing the High Priest. He scrutinized the religious man for a moment, then laughed. With a powerful, low, and chilling voice, the Prince proclaimed, "I am God!"

He turned back to the curtains and yanked them apart. He hesitated for only a moment, then marched up to the mercy seat. He sat down on the mercy seat while the room filled with reporters and soldiers. Slowly, the Prince spoke, "I am God! I am the great King who was dead and now lives! All will worship me. All will follow me. I am the messiah, the savior of mankind. You will worship no other god but me! I am the Christ!"

I bowed down on one knee. Everyone in the room followed suit. "Praise to the king. Praise to our messiah," chanted our group.

The last glimmer of sunlight passed through the park and onto the tops of the surrounding buildings. Jacob glanced at his watch. "Oh my, it's already seven, come on kids, it's getting late."

Sveta began cleaning up their picnic area as Paul and Natasha ran in with the ball they were throwing.

"Dad," Paul asked, "can we go out for some ice-cream?"

"Well, we need to go home and get some rest," Jacob answered.

"May Natasha and I go? We'll be back before nine," Paul pleaded.

"Sure, but we have no money to give you," Jacob replied.

"I have just enough for two small ones." Paul said.

Jacob smiled. "See you at home."

"All right," the kids echoed, running through the park towards the business district.

Jacob and Sveta casually walked towards the bus stop holding hands, gazing at the setting sun. As they reached the bus stop, an older lady hurried over and set a suitcase down.

"Leaving town?" Jacob asked with a smile.

"I'm getting out of the country while I can!" She replied.

"Why, what's wrong?" Sveta caringly questioned.

"Didn't you hear about the Federation?" The lady asked with surprise.

"No we've been out all afternoon," Jacob replied.

"They're taking over! The Prince flew in this afternoon with more soldiers, missiles, planes and ships. He took our Prime Minister as hostage and threatened to begin an all out attack if we didn't turn the government over to him."

"Oh my, the children!" Sveta exclaimed.

"But that's not the worst of it. The Prince went to the temple and marched into the Holiest of Holies. He declared himself God!"

"No! It couldn't happen this fast!" Jacob screamed.

"The children, we have to get the children!" Sveta exclaimed.

"Here comes a bus. I hope it will stop. God be with you," the lady said, picking up her suitcase.

"What do we do?" Sveta asked crying.

"Jesus said we have to run right away, honey." Jacob stated. "The kids know what to do. They know we will meet later."

"We don't have any clothes, food or money. We need to go back and pick up necessities," Sveta responded.

The lady at the bus shouted, "Hey, this bus is going to Jordan, you two coming?"

"We have to go, Sveta. God will watch over the family," Jacob said as he grabbed her hand.

They ran up to the bus, "Sir, we have no money with us."

"Don't worry," The bus driver said. "Hurry up and get on, we're getting out of here."

Paul and Natasha walked down the street as several people hurried by.

"It's odd." Paul stated. "A lot of people seem to be hurrying on a Sunday night."

They walked up to the ice cream shop's doors. "Why is it closed?" Natasha asked

"I don't know," Paul answered. "Let's ask someone."

A frightened man rushed by. Paul shouted to him. "Sir, what is going on?"

The man stopped. "Haven't you heard?"

"No."

"The Federation has taken over our country and the Prince declared himself God inside the temple," he said.

"Oh no!" Paul exclaimed. "Dad was right."

"Son, you two get out of here as fast as you can," the man shouted, hurrying away.

"Thanks!" Paul shouted back.

"I think we should run like dad said." Natasha stated.

"But they may be waiting at home for us, besides I have some things I want to get," Paul replied.

"But dad said to run and meet later when this happened," Natasha mentioned.

"It'll only take a little bit to get home and see if they're home," Paul said. "Besides, do you want to go without other clothes?"

"No, but let's hurry," she answered.

After the Prince allowed us to stop praising him, he ordered the reporters to leave. He instructed some of his commanders in more maneuvers and returned to me. "Joseph, bring the High Priest to me."

"Yes, sir," I replied.

I went out into the court and ordered the High Priest to go in to the King. He walked up to the spread curtains and stopped.

"I cannot enter this place without the proper cleansing, even if the Prince has desecrated it." The High Priest snarled.

"Come in and bow before me." The King commanded.

"Never!" He sternly replied.

"Kill him!" the King said.

I drew my pistol from its holster, pointed it at the High Priest's chest and hesitated only for a moment. I must obey my King. I pulled the trigger, feeling my hand jerk as the bullet hit the designated mark.

The King continued with no signs of remorse, barking out more orders. "As soon as President Carlos secures all appointed military posts, begin our next phase of operations: Eradicate the Jews!"

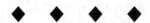

Paul and Natasha ran into the darkened apartment fumbling for the switch.

"They're gone already!" Natasha shrieked.

"Well, let's get our things packed and leave," Paul said. "See if you can find a note or something while I gather some supplies."

"Here's a note from Tim," Natasha shouted from the kitchen.

"Read it," Paul said, running into the room.

"Dear family. I've waited for almost 3 hours since the Prince desecrated our temple but don't want to wait any longer. I grabbed some extra clothes and food for everyone. The Feldblum family is coming to pick me up. Word has it that there is an air lift starting south of the city. The Lord be with you! Tim."

"Wow, that was almost six hours ago. We better move fast," Paul remarked.

Paul found some bags and began stuffing them with food, while Natasha searched for flashlights, tissue and other necessities. Paul was finishing off the second sack when a machine gun blasted near their building.

"Paul!" Natasha screamed. "They're beginning to shoot."

"It's almost midnight, we'll have to run instead of taking a bus," Paul exclaimed.

"But I can't carry more than two bags." Natasha said holding back the tears. More gunshots could be heard around the city.

"Put on a couple pairs of clothes and let's go," Paul ordered.

They raced out the door and down the steps. When they reached the front door, Paul stopped and slowly peered out. "Okay, let's go." He flung open the door and they ran to the corner.

"Hey you Jewish kids, Stop!" A loud male voice commanded.

Day 1261

The King picked up his red line phone. "Yes, President Carlos. Secure the outposts as fast as you can. Shoot some missiles into their strongholds if we have to. The faster we move the better. Good. Yes, I've been hearing the gunshots, like music to my ears. Don't worry about the ones remaining inside, we can find them later. Just kill those who flee now. Once we gain total control of the country, we will begin eliminating those who refuse to worship me."

I watched the fire in his eyes as he spoke of the extermination of the Jewish race. Hanging up the phone, he turned to me and I felt the blackness in his pupils explore into my very soul. He could sense my growing fear, and seemed to want to explore my weakness. The reassurances of the past were quickly forgotten.

"Joseph, bring the priests up to me," the King ordered. "If they will bow before me, they may serve in my presence. If not, kill them immediately."

"Yes, sir," I replied, quickly walking to the guarded priests gathered in the outer court.

I explained their choices clearly and ordered them into a single file before the King. As each one denied the deity of the King, a guard would thrust his bayonet into his heart. After the line was depleted, the king commanded for the Israeli television and radio reporters to meet him for a national speech to be broadcasted throughout the day.

"To the nation of Israel!" the King began his speech with a smile, perched triumphantly on his throne. "I am your messiah who has come to reign in the Holy City, Jerusalem. The entire world has come in peace to worship me in unity as the new age dawns on this glorious nation. Will you be a part of this exciting, fulfilled time? We can not have a peaceful earth, unless all will worship the one true God, your King! Make your decision now, worship me and live, or suffer the consequences of rejection."

As the bus rambled down the rocky road toward the Jordanian border, Jacob and Sveta discussed with the other passengers the reason for fleeing the country. All of the passengers explained their experiences of meeting two men who warned them to leave Jerusalem when the temple was invaded. Several mentioned, quite bravely, that they believed Jesus Christ was the Messiah and He was coming to rescue them in the future. The conversation centered around the two old prophets in tattered clothes.

The driver interrupted the excited conversation. "Okay, everyone, start praying. The border check is just ahead."

The group bowed in silent prayer, calling upon the protection of Jehovah.

"Oh no." The driver exclaimed. "They are all Federation soldiers."

"Maybe you should just go through at full speed!" shouted one of the passengers.

The bus driver began slowing down, not hearing the advice. The three Federation soldiers holding machine guns, continued to talk to each other and look off into the distance as the bus came to a stop. Jacob carefully watched the soldiers who seemed not to notice their presence. After a moment of hesitation, the driver jammed the gearshift in with a loud grinding noise. Jacob instinctively crouched down in his seat waiting for the soldiers reaction. The bus drove across the opened gate and into Jordan. The Jordan soldiers walked out in their path with guns pointing at the driver.

"Where are you from?" Jacob heard the soldier ask the driver.

"We are from Israel," the driver stuttered.

"Are there only Jewish people on your bus?" he asked.

"Um, yes, officer," the driver nervously answered.

The group continued praying fervently, not knowing what to expect.

"I have been ordered," the soldier exclaimed, "to allow you safe passage to a city in the south. You must make a right at the intersection ahead and follow to the next check point. You may proceed."

The stunned driver again put the bus in gear and drove away with a loud, "Thank you!"

The passengers sat in a bewildered silence for several minutes as the bus turned right down the highway. Then they all threw their arms up, breaking into cheers and hugging each other.

"God is protecting us to Petra," Jacob mumbled to himself.

Paul and Natasha hurried around the corner of the building as the man shouted, "Stop, or I'll shoot!"

They ran through the alley and around another corner towards a group of buildings. The sound of the boots running through the alley frightened Natasha into tears.

"The bags are too heavy," she screamed at Paul who was several steps ahead.

"Come on just around the building and we can get away." Paul answered puffing.

Natasha watched Paul run around the corner and stepped to follow when she heard the shot. One bag of food was yanked from her hand. The bullet imbedded into the back wall. Without stopping, she followed Paul around another corner and into another alley. They stopped for a moment to catch their breath.

"Let's stay in the dark part and we should be able to get out to that air lift," Paul stated.

"I can't run as fast with this bag," Natasha gasped. "You have to wait for me."

"Well, get rid of it," Paul quipped.

"No, it's got some personal things I need," answered Natasha.

The click of boots walking in the street shortened their rest. Jumping up, they ran through the alley towards the next street. Paul's bag bounced off a trash can, tipping it over with a loud crash. They reached the corner and stepped around into the street. A block away, two Federation soldiers stood looking at them. Paul turned for another alley and Natasha raced behind.

"Hey, you kids, shouldn't be out so late," one of the soldiers snarled, pointing his gun.

They ducked into the alley. "Take a left into the market and we'll lose them for sure," Paul gasped to Natasha.

Natasha saw the many carts and stands just ahead past the wall. Before Paul turned, Natasha heard the shot and instantaneously felt the impact of the bullet like a sledge hammer hit her in the back. She fell forward blacking out as her head slammed into the concrete.

"No!" Paul screamed dropping the bags and turning around to see the stream of blood gush from his sister.

Before the tears could form, another shot rang out and Paul was thrown to the ground by the force of the bullet ripping into his arm. He winced from the excruciating pain when he tried to move. He opened his eyes to see the bearded Federation soldier walking toward him.

The officer stopped and pointed his gun. "Still alive you Jewish brat?"

Paul didn't feel the second bullet as the blackness surrounded him.

Day 1271

I stood outside the temple in the courtyard, watching the dark storm clouds rolling. When the first bolt of lightening struck nearby, I decided to move back by the king. He was still furious about the loss of thousands of Federation troops sent to destroy the fleeing Jews.

"You mean to say, General Carlos, that our radar never picked up any of the planes and helicopters taking off? How is it that our guards never saw any of the thousands of vehicles that Jordan says passed over our borders?" the king asked shaking his head. "I see, what was the total troop loss? Over twenty thousand. No one has seen or heard from any of them? They just disappeared in the desert in hot pursuit of the fleeing Jews? It's incredible. Wait, I have an idea. We can tell the media how we allowed the Jews free passage if they didn't want to stay. Don't mention our losses. How is the second attack on Petra going? What? Right now? I hate the Jews and their God!"

The king slammed down the phone. "Colonel, is it true that there is hail, lightening and blood pouring from the skies?"

"Yes, sir," he replied, "there are reports of fires all around the world. The blood is coming down like rain and has stopped all movement of transportation."

"That does it," the king stated sarcastically. "I want you to implement my program of genocide of all the Jews and their disgusting gentile proselytes, those who believe in Jesus, from all nations, immediately!"

The cliffs along the narrow passage ascended into the heavens. Occasionally the sun would pass over the rocks creating dazzling images of color painted on the walls. Everyone with Jacob and Sveta walked slowly admiring the natural beauty. Jacob led the group single file as they approached the ancient city of Petra.

The giant columns upon the opposite cliff face revealed the end of the small passage. Jacob walked out of the opening into the great city of rock, Petra. The group gathered behind him sputtering utterances of amazement.

"It's entirely carved out from the rock cliffs," Sveta gasped.

The city buzzed with activity like the first day at a national convention. People with suitcases hustled back and forth, vendors shouted about their goods. Thousands stood alone in an open area, holding signs with names of family members for whom they were waiting.

Another group pushed Jacob's group from behind emerging from the passageway. Jacob and Sveta began looking for their children as they walked down the dusty rock floor where the canyon broadened into a wide expanse. A uniformed military man shouted out with a speaker for all newcomers to register before setting up residence.

They walked to the back of the lines of families registering. Jacob could not believe the thousands of people waiting. He counted thirty separate lines with at least one hundred persons each. He shook his head and sat down on the ground preparing for the wait.

After five long hours, Jacob and Sveta finally approached the registration desk. Every fifteen minutes or so, an Israeli officer would explain the procedures through his speaker phone. His voice echoed off the towering rock walls.

The tall, dark captain began, "On behalf of the few government officials who made the journey to Petra safely, we praise God for your arrival. Please understand the difficulties we face. We've already admitted over two hundred thousand and expect over a million more, once our people get word of where to go. Currently, the officials who have escaped are seeking to establish some sort of rule that the remaining military has pledged to employ. The current program is as follows: First, only those who are in line may register. All of us have missing family, so expect a couple of weeks to be reunited, do not register anyone not with you in line. Second, after registering you may begin your search for shelter. If you find an empty living area you may claim it as the primary family. Later, others will be added to your place to meet the need for shelter. We expect a minimum of eight per shelter and possibly more. Those with tents may erect them in the designated tent cities. One family member must remain in the shelter at all times until further notice. In approximately two weeks, we will conduct a census and carry forth the ruling legislation to inform you of the new laws to be implemented for peaceful community living. We will then begin the process of permanent location based on order of registration. It will be to your advantage to fill each shelter with maximum occupancy of your own choosing. Until then, any peace breakers will be held in a temporary military prison camp. Please, follow the old law of helping each other. We must stay united during this emergency situation. Thank you.

Jacob stepped up to the table and registered himself and Sveta. He asked about his family, but the soldier behind the desk laughed. He answered. "It would be impossible to tell you if they were here. Look at this mess. Just go find a place to stay until they can be located later."

Jacob grabbed Sveta's hand and walked past the table. "Let's pray that we can find the kids soon." Jacob began, "Lord, we thank you again for the safe passage to Petra. We pray that Paul, Timothy and Natasha will find their way safely. We ask for your help in finding our children, and your leading in where to go now. We look for your soon return, Lord Jesus. Please save our people. It's through you that we pray. Amen."

"Dad!" Jacob heard Tim's voice.

Tim ran up and hugged Sveta and then Jacob as he cried with joy. "I've been praying ever since I left."

"We've been praying for you the whole time," Jacob said with tears in his eyes.

"Are Paul and Natasha here?" Sveta asked.

"I haven't seen them, but that's not saying much. It's a mad house. I've been waiting for five hours. They could be anywhere."

"Have you been waiting here since you came?"

"No, the Solomon's and I arrived late last night and were able to find a really good place. It's got a view down the canyon and enough room for both families. I slept a little and then came down here."

"We haven't slept a wink," Sveta explained. "We didn't even have time to go home. Once we heard about the Prince, we took the next bus."

"Well, don't worry," Tim said with a smile. "I had time to get pillows, blankets and some clothes for everyone. We even had enough room in the van for some extra food and supplies."

"That's great. You are a good son," Jacob and Sveta chorused.

Tim turned and led them towards their new home discussing all the events of the trip.

Day 1278

The Pope's arrival in Jerusalem brought hundreds of thousands of curious onlookers to the streets for the big parade. I, of course, stayed in the temple next to the King awaiting his arrival. The King already explained to me what events would happen. We patiently waited for the Pope to come into the temple and begin the proceedings.

His submission and subsequent worship of the King would bring the last major group of people in the world to the King's feet. Atheist and agnostics have acknowledged the deity of the King already. The Muslims, though a part of the World Church, have overwhelmingly supported the King's throne because of the return of Israel back to their people. Tens of thousands of Muslims arrive everyday in Israel, replacing the deceased Jewish residents. I think most people in the World Church already followed our King, but the Pope's approval will convince all believers that the Christ has arrived and we now will live in peace and harmony under the rule of our great King.

I watched the Pope enter through the curtains and approach the King who stood up from the throne. The Pope fell to his knees and worshiped, saying, "The Christ is come! All must worship the King, our savior."

The new temple priests brought a lamb to the altar in front of the temple. The Pope again commanded all people to worship the King as he lifted his hands above his head. A giant column of fire descended to the altar consuming the lamb. Everyone, including myself, fell down before the King giving him praise, though I did keep my eyes open still doing my duty. Afterwards, the Pope began healing people from every physical malady imaginable. He was so humble when people offered him praise, he ordered them to only praise the King.

As the day came to a close the guards dismissed the crowd from the temple grounds. They took their positions outside the exterior walls. Three familiar hooded figures entered with the Austrian President and approached the King. One by one they bowed before him and took positions around the throne facing the King. Each one lit an incense candle and placed it on the ground in front of themselves, while kneeling down. I followed the cue of the Pope and dropped to my knee before the King.

In his usual, calm voice he began, "Doesn't it feel good to be in the middle of our enemy's house, worshiping me in the victory of conquering the enemy's land?"

"Yes. Yes. Praise the King. Yes, praise the King." the group chanted.

"Speak out all of you!" The King commanded.

A chorus of unearthly, deep, raspy voices burst out all around the room. "We worship you, Satan. You are the supreme being. You are conqueror and victorious."

The fear welled up within my stomach spreading outward to my extremities. I began to shake uncontrollably. I collapsed with a whimper onto the ground curling into a fetal position, still convulsing.

I heard the King continue as if nothing were amiss, "the trinity is complete. We are together. Satan our Father, myself the Christ, and now the spirit, the Great Prophet. We hold all power, we are invincible on earth. However, our task is not complete. To totally defeat our enemy, we must destroy His people on earth!"

"Death to the Jews," The voices chorused.

"We will finish the work on our androids and implement my mark in the coming weeks! We will destroy the World Church and bring its money to me to be divided. I will unveil my new laws for our world and you will be the supreme commanders. The current task is to gather our angels and people to hunt, seek and destroy the enemy!"

"Destroy the Jews!"

"My angel, the great Prince of Persia, has chosen this human to dwell in as needed. He will command our angelic army."

I felt a great pain in my insides. My brain burned with electrical charges. I jumped to my feet with no control of what I was doing. Every muscle in my body flexed and shook with a power unimaginable. I picked up the machine gun lying at my feet and began bending the steel nozzle with my bare hands. As the steel broke in half in my hands, I looked up into the faces of the most horrific creatures. For a brief moment I saw their extended claws, disfigured faces and the bloody fangs as they began laughing. A deep, thick fog covered my eyes, and laughter faded into the distance.

Tim picked up the latest news release from the army guard table after waiting in line for half an hour to receive the one page report. He pushed his way through the crowded street constantly watching for any signs of his siblings. As he moved away from the most congested areas and into the more open expanse, he stopped by one of the many tents to read the sheet. Finishing, he folded the paper, put it into his pocket and continued towards his new home in the cliff walls. He passed by the giant Roman theater which the army used every evening for troop coordinators and information. They allowed anyone to come and listen to the latest reports, but Tim had grown weary of fighting the crowds to even get within ear shot of the briefings. It was easier just to listen to the others who had attended explain what had been stated. As he made his way up the steep embankments towards home, Tim stopped for a moment to gaze down upon the wondrous valley. The crowds could be seen throughout the center of this strange city through which he had just come.

The walls stretched hundreds of feet into the air above the dusty floor below which pulsated with life as the renewed center of Petra. The passage opened slowly into the valley with openings which appeared like honeycombs on the sides of the reddish-rock hills. Many other stone buildings including the Roman theater were scattered about. The entire valley was enclosed by mountains, the tallest being Aaron's mount, over 5000 feet tall. The only way into the valley was through the small southern crevice through which Jacob and his family had come, or by plane to the newly constructed runway. Traveling over the mountains was possible, but very treacherous. Tim finished his viewing by admiring the planes used in the airlift. God miraculously caused Jordan to build an airport recently, allowing the Jews to airlift from Israel into Petra. Tim truly was amazed by God's wonderful fore-knowledge. He climbed the remaining steps and ran into the opening of the rock which was their home.

"It's been a week, where are they?" Sveta sat crying with her hand buried in her hands. "We should have found them by now."

"There are two million people here, they could be anywhere," Jacob reassured.

"Mom, Dad!" Tim shouted. "Here's the latest news from army headquarters."

"Thanks," Jacob said taking the flyer.

"It says they will start the census and put up the list of the ones who have registered."

"Good, we can check if Paul and Natasha have registered," Jacob stated hopefully. "Does it say anything more about the fires?"

"No, but everyone is saying that one-third of all trees in the world were destroyed and there is no more green grass anywhere. Some are even saying it rained blood."

"No...that's disgusting...I doubt if it's true." Sveta said.

"I'm not sure either, but God sure has protected us here," Jacob stated looking out across the flowery valley. "I need to get back to reading the Bible. I know it has the answers!"

Day 1290

I stared at the perfectly-formed android with amazement.

Even though I knew all about the Pope's masterpiece, the sight of it, as he pulled the sheets off the nine foot tall scientific wonder, left me breathless. How could it look just like the King?

The gathered crowd of reporters cheered and marveled as the android spoke in a deep, perfectly matched voice of the King, "You will worship me. I am the great King. I have risen from the dead. Bow down before me."

I quickly dropped to my knees with the other guards as we had been ordered. With my head slightly down in a bowed position, I continued to observe the room. Almost everyone followed our cue and fell to their knees, but a few foolish reporters hurriedly jotted notes. The android fixed his eyes upon the first reporter. I couldn't see the laser burn into the reporter's nerve, but I know it was working. The man clutched his chest and fell to the ground dead. The two other rebellious reporters died in the same manner. The android repeated his command with even more authority, "Fall down and worship me or die!"

The Pope then stepped back to the microphone. "Tomorrow at noon, all will worship the King and his image. Please tune in your televisions to any channel for the broadcast. The King demands all citizens of the world unite in worship, in order to bring in our new age."

I stepped up next to the King as the other body guards ushered the reporters out of the temple.

"Is everything ready?" the King asked.

"The computers are set and ready. We can do the broadcast and begin the marking of our followers," the Pope replied.

"Good. My time has finally come. After all these years, my plan has taken effect, I've spent years promoting my propaganda of the New World Order. All the cartoons, magazines, movies and politicians I've put in place to slowly capture the hearts of all men. I am the one all religions have prophesied would come to bring in the new age, utopia and heaven on earth. Billions of souls will unite in peace as they focus all worship upon me. I am the world's savior. I myself, am the greatest power in the universe. No one can fathom the depth of my wisdom and knowledge. Even Daniel's wisdom was as foolishness compared to me. Who will dare to stand before me?"

"My angels obey each command proceeding from my mouth. Millions of children willingly followed my musicians in worshiping my real name, Satan. They sacrificed animals and people to me in hopes of obtaining just a glimpse of my awesome power. Those who would not willingly follow, I deceived with all subtleness, every year filtering my wonderful wisdom into their puny brains through the media. Now, they willingly bow before me and my image the prophet has created. Our enemy and His pitiful army of misfits cannot stand before our trinity: The father, Satan; His son, the King; and the spirit, our Great Prophet. We have taken the earth, and the people have given it to us. Those who will not worship me, I will destroy! I am the future. I will beat our enemy, the God of the Jews!"

As the King spoke, I slowly felt my senses disappearing. My whole body tingled, as if every joint had fallen asleep. All at once a sharp pain shot from my stomach into my throat. I heard myself speaking in another language with great veracity. I couldn't stop the words which ferociously flowed with increasing intensity, nor my body as it bowed to the King. I had no control.

Jacob and Tim silently ascended the cliffs toward home. Jacob had dreaded the reaction of Sveta once she learned that Paul and Natasha did not make it. He worried that she might go into a frenzy and begin running around the city searching, or worse, decide to venture back to Jerusalem.

Sveta was waiting in the makeshift living room with the Solomons. The instant Jacob and Tim walked in, she knew the news. "Well, there's still a chance that they found a hiding place in Jerusalem or the countryside," she said before Jacob could say anything.

The three of them came together and wept while embracing. "We still have to pray for them, just in case," Sveta cried.

"We will, dear," Jacob assured.

After some time together praying with the Solomons, they all walked out into the valley to gather food for supper. The bountiful berries and nuts were plucked and put into baskets. No one dared to talk, choosing to pray silently instead. They finished gathering and brought the food home to eat.

Before they gave thanks for the food, Sveta spoke. "I really appreciate the love we are sharing during this time. It means so much to me to have such a wonderful family and friends. But it's time to move on. I have given Paul and Natasha back to God. I am assured that they truly accepted Jesus as the only Messiah. If they are still alive, only Jesus can protect them. If the Father has seen fit to take them to heaven, they are much better off anyway."

Jacob smiled and gave thanks for the food. Everyone started eating, and the conversation began with the rumor about the android and the coming identification mark. Jacob looked at his wife who was eating and participating in the discussion. He marveled at his wife's growing strength in the Lord.

Her eyes were sparkling from the fountain of faith bubbling up from deep within her soul. God's abundant grace was shining from his own wife. She glanced at Jacob and flashed a warm smile. Jacob felt strength through Sveta's yielding to God's perfect will. Jacob smiled back. He felt the heavy burden of Paul and Natasha lifting off his heart. He was giving them both to God.

Day1320

The King slowly walked toward the fully decorated general in his accusatory way. His nostrils flared slightly as he spoke in a low, raspy voice. Tell me again, general, how did we lose one hundred thousand troops, and thousands of military vehicles?"

The stout general swallowed hard and responded with a cracking voice, "Your Majesty, I have gone over every conceivable explanation. The results indicate a supernatural event of some sort. We finished with positioning all ground troops outside the valley and dispatched the air forces just as you ordered. Seconds before the air strike was about to begin we lost all contact with both ground and air personnel. Our reports confirmed a giant sand storm engulfed the entire army. Everything and everyone vanished with no trace."

The King continued walking to the general, pausing for a moment as he stepped in front of him. Sweat droplets formed quickly on the general's forehead as the King glared down into his eyes.

"I do not tolerate incompetence!" The King shouted. He took his hand and clasped the general's neck, lifting him with one arm. As the general gasped for air and tried to struggle free, the King continued, "When I sent one hundred thousand of our best troops to kill the Jews still hiding in Petra, I thought I would send the best general I had to lead them in a victory of magnificent proportions. Instead you not only lost everything, you disgraced my name. If you had won, you could have reigned third in command of the entire world army. Instead your failure to me has caused your own demise. I accept nothing less than total victory!"

With that the King squeezed his hand, crushing the neck with a blood curdling crack. He dropped the once colorful general into a heap on the floor.

Turning around, he began talking to the Prophet in his normal voice as if nothing happened. "How is the final day for receiving my identification panning out?"

"Just as you ordered. We have counted almost four billion worshipers total having received one of the symbols this month. Beginning tomorrow, no one will be able to buy or sell anything without it, under penalty of death," the Prophet answered.

"Great," the King stated looking out his window. "The enemy must be disgusted with what His creation is doing. They will bow and worship me at my bidding. Now, we must command their loyalty for the war ahead. I will lead them in battle against the God of the Jews for our planet!"

The Solomons, Rubensteins and two other couples sat in the front room of the cave home. Several lanterns hung on the walls, giving light to the three opened Bibles. Jacob sat in the only wooden chair with his Bible open in his lap. A stack of notes lay next to the chair within his arm-reach. All eyes and ears focused upon Jacob after he finished praying out loud.

"I want to say thank you for the opportunity to speak forth God's Word to you. It has been exciting to live here with the Solomons and be a part of their new-found faith in Israel's only Messiah, Jesus. Equally enjoyable, has been God's leading in meeting the Wilkinsons and Goldsteins, who also became Believers before the flight to Petra. My faith has grown incredibly this last month and I am encouraged that all of us want to meet every night and study God's Word. Right now, I am honored to teach what I've been studying before our flight and especially these past few weeks. God is revealing more and more to me as I pray for guidance."

"Tonight, I thought we would study about what happened three and a half years ago. The Bible has many references to the disappearance, or new beginning, to coin a phrase, of the Prince.

In Genesis chapter five, verse twenty four, we read that Enoch was taken by God and did not die. It should be noted that the judgment of the flood happened after Enoch was taken off the earth. In Revelation chapter four, verses one and two, we read that the disciple John was translated up to heaven from earth after the Lord called him. Again, the judgments in Revelation occur after John is called to heaven. Jesus said in Matthew chapter twenty four that His coming would be just like in the days of Noah.

In First Corinthians, chapter fifteen, verses fifty one through fifty three, Paul tells us how this change will happen in a twinkling of an eye. He also wrote in First Thessalonians, chapter four, the exact events that would occur during this brief moment of translating Believers from earth into Heaven.

I believe what was first called a "disappearance", then later phrased "the new beginning", was actually Jesus calling His people up to Heaven! Let us look at these, and other passages, more closely to determine what really happened a few years ago."

Day 1350

The King and I sat in his office watching the news report of the latest catastrophe. I couldn't believe that one-third of the oceans turned to blood. What a horrific sight!

"Please call a press conference." The King spoke to his secretary through the intercom.

After a few phone calls, we walked down to the press area for the speech. He jumped up into the podium and immediately began venting his anger towards the Jews and their God.

"Whom do you want to serve? A God who destroys and ruins the earth, or one who has given you freedom? It is because of my new Bill of Commandments that this jealous, Jewish God wishes to bring harm to our precious planet. His people, the Jews, want to obey His oppressive laws and ten commandments. They proclaim themselves better than the rest of us. My new Bill of Commandments bring freedom, equality, peace and the right for you to pursue every pleasure. His commands bring guilt, oppression and prejudice between ethnic groups. To eliminate Him, we must eliminate His people. Death to the Jews! Help us find them, call your local King's Force station with any details. We must protect mother earth!"

"Dad!" Tim shouted, running into the cave house. "One-third of the oceans turned to blood!"

"Where did you hear it?" Jacob asked with raised eyebrows.

"It's on the latest news release from army headquarters. It says the King is blaming us and our God."

Jacob nodded his head. "Well, if there was any doubt before, about the Bible's predictions, this puts them to rest. This event is described precisely in Revelation eight, verses eight and nine which we have been studying."

"What's next?" Sveta asked walking into the room.

"Let's see here," Jacob responded, picking up the Bible. "In verse ten and eleven it says the Lord will send a star from heaven called wormwood and one-third of the rivers and fountains of water will become poisoned. Many people will die from it."

"Oh no. How will we be able to drink anything?" Sveta questioned with worry in her voice.

"Actually, I've just started to study about us Jews here at Petra," Jacob said with a smile. "I think we are going to be totally protected."

"What?" Sveta and Tim optimistically questioned. They both sat down and eagerly waited for Jacob's reasons.

"Yes. I was going to begin this for our Bible study in the next few days."

"Tell us now," Sveta and Tim chorused.

"You know how we've been studying the disappearance and this tribulation period? I think I've found more verses about our people." Jacob stated pulling out some notes and flipping through the Bible. "I'll show you a few of the major ones now."

Jacob glanced at his notes and began. "The first reference is in Genesis chapter seven, with Noah. He was the great grandson of Enoch. He took his family into the ark, and they were protected by God from the flood. Jesus mentioned this in Matthew when he warned of the coming judgment. In Exodus, our people were miraculously protected from the judgments God sent into Egypt. Every plague including hail, blood, darkness and death.

"That's exactly what Revelation predicts!" Timothy exclaimed.

"Right," replied Jacob. "We can't explain how God can cause the whole world to be plagued, but keep Petra protected. No one in Egypt could explain how the land of Goshen could escape the plagues, except a miracle. When our people did leave Egypt, God provided food and protection for forty years. There were six hundred thousand men and even more women and children."

"Do you think," Tim asked, "that the reason for all the water and food we have in Petra is similar to that of Israel in the wilderness?"

"Yes," Jacob answered. "We have escaped the King, like Israel escaped Pharaoh. We are safely in a wilderness while the world is being judged. We continue to have plenty of food and water, even though Petra has been a desert. We don't have any meat, just like Israel complained about in Numbers chapter eleven."

"In other words," Sveta stated. "God has miraculously saved a remnant of His chosen race, protecting and nourishing us while we wait in Petra for Jesus' return as our King."

"Exactly!" Jacob exclaimed. "In Matthew chapter twenty four, Jesus prophesied about our people. He warned us when the abomination of desolation occurred, to run to the mountains. Petra is surrounded by the highest mountains anywhere near Israel. Then our people would be slaughtered unlike anytime before. We know the Prince has already murdered millions more than Hitler did. Then Jesus said after the great tribulation, He would come in the clouds of heaven with power and glory."

"Is He coming at the very end of the great tribulation?" Tim asked.

"Yes," replied Jacob. "In chapter twelve of Revelation, God speaks of Israel bringing forth the Messiah. Then the Messiah would ascend to His throne, while Israel would flee to the wilderness for exactly one thousand two hundred and sixty days. It again states that Satan would try to kill us, but God would protect and nourish us for three and a half years. Then Satan would go out and kill as many Jews as he can, who did not make it here."

"What happens at the end of the three and a half years?" Sveta questioned.

"To begin with," Jacob started, "let me read in Revelation nineteen..."

Day 1620

I peered down at the resume, focusing my eyes in the diminished light from the office lamp. It's difficult to find credible replacements for the King's personal bodyguard. We are still one short of full staff, but I must hire only someone who is qualified, willing to give his life for the King, and able to work extensive hours. Only five applicants have been chosen out of the thousands received, to replace the six that died three months ago from the poisoned water.

The King overheard my mumbling as I shuffled through the latest stack of top applications sent by the executive secretary. "Having a hard time finding our last replacement?" the King asked.

"Uh, yes sir. I only want the absolute best."

The King stopped for a moment and shut his eyes. "Take the first one in this next stack," he ordered and went back to his notes.

Instantly, the secretary walked through the door with another handful of papers. "Here, Mr. Van Buren."

"Thank you," I replied taking the top resume and tossing the others into the trash can. She looked at me with surprise, then shrugged her shoulders and walked back out the door.

"Here it comes," the King spoke into the intercom as the sunlight burst through the windows recovering from the strange blockage of the past eight hours. "Now get me a reason from one of our satellites immediately!"

Within minutes, the intercom buzzed. "Your Highness, from all the data we have received there is no explanation. The computers specify a dark void four hours east and west of the world's sunrise permitting neither sunlight nor starlight penetration. We are sending satellite video into your receiver now."

I jumped up and opened the oak cabinet doors revealing the giant television screen. I stepped back in amazement, viewing the colorful earth with the strange block of darkness covering one-third of the sunlight.

"Humph," the King snorted. "I like the darkness better anyway. Let's go Joseph. We have a meeting to attend."

Jacob sat in the doorway of his cave house, with his Bible open in one hand and his head buried in the other as he finished praying. Looking upon the group of fifty or so gathered around the rocky ledge for their nightly Bible study, a broad grin spread across his face. The Bible study group had outgrown the living room two months prior, even with the meetings every night. For three days he spoke the same lesson, with a new lesson following the next three days. It seemed the Lord continued to add people each day, not only to Jacob's Bible study, but to the twenty other groups meeting throughout Petra. But with the growth, also came the opposition. Many orthodox priests and devout Jews would throw stones at the gathered groups, shouting, "Only Jehovah lives!" Sometimes they would convince soldiers to help break up a study on a given night. Other times, the soldiers listened to the speaker proclaiming God's Word and helped protect them instead.

The designated military leaders refused to take sides. They allowed the orthodox priests to continue their meetings on the Sabbath (though the sacrifices haven't been continued due to the loss of the proper equipment and the lack of any proper animals with which to perform the ceremony). They allow freedom for citizens to debate who might be the Messiah. The greatest majority of the army and the two million citizens of Petra remained confused about the whole ordeal.

Jacob began by reading First Corinthians chapter eleven. He also read several passages in the Gospels.

"It is good to have so many present to hear the words of our Lord, Jehovah. For those who are new, please remain afterwards and set up a weekly time with Mark Solomon or Jim Wilkinson or myself. We will joyfully answer your questions and catch you up on our previous studies."

"Recently we have studied how Jesus Christ fulfilled all the requirements of Old Testament prophecies concerning the Messiah. We looked at His sinless life and humbleness, even to a torturous death on the cross. We proved His resurrection and the start of the church, which includes Gentiles and Hebrews alike. Before we begin the study about our current events and what is to come, I want to present ideas about our fellowship together and worship of God."

"In the passages we just read, Jesus commands us to break bread and drink the fruit of the vine in remembrance of His death. As we have studied, Jesus fulfilled all the sacrifices of the law with His own perfect sacrifice of Himself for our sins. There is no need for further sacrifice for our sin. However, Jesus wanted us to remember the only payment of sin, His death, until He returns as the King of Israel. Though we are looking for Jesus to come again and set up His Kingdom in Jerusalem, I think we are obligated to continue worshiping Him by remembering His death as the church of both the Jews and Gentiles did before us."

"In discussions with Mark and Jim, we've decided to host an open meeting with believers in Christ to remember the Lord Jesus with breaking of bread and drinking of new wine. All believers are encouraged to prepare and come this Sabbath at sunrise for our first gathering in the name of the Lord Jesus. We will continue to hold these nightly Bible studies as well as our daily times with others. Beginning next week, we will embark on a current events study to proclaim the Messiah Jesus and prove to the remaining Jews in Petra that this time is predicted throughout the Bible. Those believing in the Kingdom of Jesus Christ will be encouraged to come to the weekly worship meeting."

"Please turn with me to Acts and focus on how the New Testament church started with the Jewish people in Jerusalem."

The King sat majestically in the Holiest of Holies with the gathered group of priests and the Prophet. He opened his mouth and a low, wicked voice almost mechanical, spoke so deep my ears hurt. "Our battle looms ahead. Preparations are being made. Abaddon is ready to lead our forces through the souls of these inferior humans. They await in the pit, seeking revenge upon earth. Soon we will gather all men to me, to fight our enemy. We will win! We will defeat Him, His angels and His disgusting human slaves! Are the kings being prepared in Persia?"

The instant the King's eyes looked into mine, my stomach and lungs seemed to burst and burn inside. I grabbed the pillar with my right arm and tried to scream in pain, instead a burning sensation shot up my throat and over my tongue. Words were being spoken through my mouth, but they weren't mine. My eyes tried to shut from the excruciating pain, but I fought with all my strength to stay coherent. My sight blurred from the massive pounding through my head, and my knees shook violently, wanting to collapse. As the fire poured out my throat, all faces turned to me. I saw within their eyes and souls the spiritual beings who controlled their human bodies.

They had faces like men, but with hard and disfigured features. Their hair was as a woman's hair, and wings rose from their backs. A tail slithered around with a stinger similar to that of a scorpions. One opened it's mouth revealing the giant teeth like that of a lion, and a forked tongue like a snake.

As my strength failed, and the blackness narrowed in, I saw the King's face. The bright glory of the creature from within him lit the room with brilliance. It was the most beautiful creature I ever looked upon.

Day 1800

The King's bodyguards stood at attention facing me as I relayed the latest orders to them. I heard a gasp from one of them and looked up from my clipboard. One of the guards stood entranced staring above me with an expression of total fear. I looked up and back, but couldn't see anything.

"No," the guard uttered, his body collapsing to the ground. He let out an ear splitting-scream and tried to gasp for air. He convulsed violently for a brief moment, then became totally motionless. As we gathered around him, two more guards screamed and fell to the floor. Seven more fell to the ground dying in the same manner. The other twenty guards frantically ran out of the room, fearing a deadly disease.

The King had already warned me, so I knew this was from the despicable God of the Jews. I looked up into the air and shook my fist with rage, "I hate You! We will defeat You!"

Timothy passed the communion cup and finished his prayer to the Lord. The four hour worship meeting passed quickly with all the different men standing up and proclaiming new insights to the Old and New Testaments about Jesus. He remembered back about five months ago when the first meeting took place inside their home.

About thirty people showed up to participate in the Lord's Supper. Only a few of the men actually stood up and spoke in the open meeting, but each had heartfelt words of worship and praise, sharing Scriptures which spoke of Jesus.

Timothy remembered how humbled he felt as they broke the unleavened bread and he envisioned Jesus' body being pierced with the nails and sword of the Roman soldiers. He could still taste the very sweet, yet bitter grape juice as the group passed the cup from one to another. Timothy realized that the juice was to remind him of the cleansing blood that Jesus shed to purify him, and all those who believe. Jesus paid the ultimate price two thousand years ago, but Timothy knew it wasn't until he accepted Jesus as the Messiah, when the two witnesses came, that the ultimate sacrifice of God's Son wiped clean the darkened sins of his life. The fact that Jesus rose again proved the certainty of the future return of Israel's King.

Timothy shook his head wondering why people were so blind. That first meeting had passed quickly in just two hours, but now, with almost one hundred in attendance, four hours seemed too short. Over twenty men stood up and proclaimed God's Word and expounded upon the deep thoughts in Scripture. None the less, the group slowly disbursed, trying to catch up on some of the recent news.

"What's the latest?" William, one of the new converts asked, knowing Timothy had a close friend in the military headquarters office staff who kept him abreast of all the world events.

"Supposedly, yesterday, over a billion people died from what they are determining as heart attacks," Timothy sadly answered.

"Wow, is that in the Bible?"

"Yes, in Revelation chapter nine, verse fifteen to the end of the chapter," Timothy replied as several more gathered around.

"So did it happen like we were studying?" Stacey, another recent convert who had fled Ethiopia asked inquisitively.

"Just like it's laid out in Scripture," Timothy nodded.

"Are there other disasters written in the Bible?" William asked.

"You bet," John, a regular to the meeting since it started, piped in, "you know the great virus they talked about that first hit five months ago? Well, it says in Revelation that it isn't a virus. We think it is actual demon attacks from the bottomless pit!"

"Wow, I just accepted Jesus as the Messiah and my own Savior a couple of weeks ago because of the testimony of a neighbor. By God's grace I met Timothy and he invited me today. But, I haven't heard about all this," William said excitedly. "What's next?"

"It says in chapter sixteen that the next worldly disaster will be horrible sores upon those who worship the King, whom we know as the anti-Christ, " Timothy said, "but we are also looking for the two witnesses in Jerusalem to be killed sometime soon."

"Yes, I remember hearing those two warn of abominations taking place in the sanctuary. That's the main reason why I ran to the air lifts, but I didn't hear much else of what they taught. Everyone laughed at them."

"That was Moses and Elijah," John interrupted.

"Really?" William questioned, opening his mouth in surprise.

"One of them could be Enoch," Timothy stated, "But most likely it is Moses and Elijah as stated in Malachi, Revelation chapter eleven and some other passages. The Bible explains that the two prophets will prophesy for three and a half years. Then Satan through the anti-Christ will kill them. We figure it could be anytime for that."

"Oh no. Satan defeats them?"

"Only for three and a half days, then God will raise them up and they will ascend to Heaven!" Timothy explained. Smiling he continued, "Don't worry, Satan's supposed victories are only temporary and God always uses them for His ultimate glory and purpose."

"What about us?" William fearfully asked. "Are we predicted in the Bible hiding here?"

"Yes, my dad is currently doing a study on our situation and is showing me some interesting passages. In the Old Testament law, God set up cities of refuge for those who killed somebody by accident or without intention. The accused person would flee to the appointed city and remain there until the death of the high priest. If he ventured forth out of the city before the appointed time, he could be avenged by the avenger. In the same way, our fathers killed the Lord Jesus and brought His blood upon our heads."

"I understand!" William exclaimed with excitement. "We are indirectly responsible for Jesus's death because our people condemned Him on the cross. We are now hiding in Petra as our city of refuge."

"Correct. In Revelation chapter twelve the Lord shows how He carried us here and will protect and nourish us for three and a half years. Do you remember the army that the Prince sent against us?"

"Sure."

"It was predicted in chapter twelve as well as how the earth would swallow up the Prince's attack."

"That explains the giant sand storm our headquarters said destroyed the Federation attack," William acknowledged with a nod of his head.

"That's only the beginning," Timothy stated, "the worst is yet to come!"

Day 1886

We watched the news cameras pan across the dusty street showing the hundreds of beggars, their bellies bloated from starvation, crying out for food. I shook my head in disgust, knowing that the three and a half years of drought was directly due to the two old men and their prophecies.

"It's time," the King said in a matter of fact voice. "Call a press conference."

The secretary quickly touched the prepared buttons and announced for all media personnel to congregate at the conference center. The King turned to Commander Carlos and signaled him to begin the prepared battle plans. The Commander nodded and walked down the hall for military headquarters.

Thirty minutes later, the King stepped boldly to the platform covered with microphones. His words came like fire with heartfelt determination. "The people of this world deserve a fruitful life, but the God of the Jews wants to hurt and destroy you. His servants must be sought out and killed. I have decided to step up our efforts in elimination of the rebels. Two of their leaders reside in the streets of Jerusalem. With my power, I will put their despicable bodies and beliefs into the grave! Pray to me and worship me, that I might save the world!'

The King wasted no time with answering questions. He ordered me to lead the way to the limo while guards marched alongside.

"Put the Commander on the speaker," the King told the driver.

The Prophet was already seated opposite the King, seemingly in deep meditation.

"Where are the two defiant ones?" the King asked.

"They are right in front of the domed worship center, next to your temple," the Commander responded, "We are positioned precisely where you mapped out, waiting for the first attack signal."

"We will be there in two minutes, wait for my signal," the King said with a snarl.

Even though I knew the plan the King had laid out, my lips trembled not knowing if I would live through the battle. I was to shield the King along with the other six chosen guards from any stray shots until King could face the two old men. The King himself seemed almost unsure of the outcome. He sat staring blankly at the great Prophet who continued to hang his head as if praying earnestly.

We stopped a block away from the King's temple and guards immediately surrounded the King. Thousands of people were gathering to see the battle and everyone who saw the King began chanting and praising His victory. We rounded the corner and beheld the two old men kneeling in the middle of the street in prayer to their God. Their darkened gray beards almost touched the ground with dirt and ashes blowing around their wrinkled faces.

They stood up, as if they knew we had come into view, with hands extended outward. The King nodded and the air was filled with tank and gun shots. The two old men seemed untouched and began breathing fire towards the surrounding army. The high pitched scream of missiles whistled overhead and balls of expanding fire engulfed the street. I shielded my face from the intense heat, with my forearm. More streams of fire retaliated above us and two guards fainted in a pool of sweat. The King tapped my shoulder and I stepped away. The great Prophet followed one step behind and to the side as they approached the wall of flames.

All at once, the gunfire and whistling ceased. The explosions continued only a moment and dissipated into a smoke cloud rising above. The streets and walls surrounding the two old men were charred in deep black. Small fires continued to burn around the untouched men with a deafening silence. The King pointed his index finger at the two old men and screamed, "In the name of world peace and the innocent lives of which you have taken, I condemn you to death!"

The great Prophet shoved his two fists into the air and the King pointed his finger at the first old man. A white light like a lightening bolt shot from his finger and blasted into the old man knocking him to the ground in a heap.

The other old man immediately said, "Oh Wicked One, you may kill our bodies now, but the Lord has reserved you for everlasting judgment. Your time is short!"

"Enough!" the King commanded as he shot another bolt of light into the second old man.

The King slowly walked over to the two bodies lying in the middle of the street. He kicked each one in the side and spit on their chests. The camera crews were already moving in to capture the triumphant moment. "I am the King! We will be victorious!"

Day 1890

"I explicitly instructed that no pictures nor articles of their resurrection would be shown to anyone!" the King angrily shouted into the phone. "I want everyone responsible for the leak to be found and executed. We will not allow false testimonies of this situation to be reported. Just mention that the bodies were disposed of and continue on with the other news. We're fortunate it never reached the mainstream press and few people read about it."

I sat back in my chair remembering how wonderful the last few days had been until today. The King announced a three day world holiday to celebrate his victory over the two old men. Everyone raucously partied and exchanged gifts with each other. The King gave me a priceless gold cup from the old Roman empire. It was a most joyous occasion.

Early this morning, while we were on our way to the temple, we stopped to view the two bodies once again. All of a sudden, the two old men stood up on their feet. Their wrinkles were gone and a sun-like glow brightened their clothes into a pure, snowy white.

A great voice from the sky shouted, "Come up here!" The two men slowly rose into the sky and disappeared into the clouds. The King stood dumbfounded with his mouth open. I began to tremble uncontrollably. Fear gripped my stomach unlike any other I've ever known. The God of the Jews can also raise people from the dead!

I walked with the King towards His temple, but before we reached the entrance, the ground started shaking. Instinctively, I wanted to cover the King, but the violent shaking buckled my knees and I fell to the ground. I could do nothing, save for grabbing the cement with my hands in hopes of retaining my balance.

When the earthquake ceased, the King commanded, "Come on Joseph, there is work to be done."

The King appeared untroubled by the event, but I was visibly upset. Even with the news of seven thousand killed and a tenth of Jerusalem destroyed, the King seemed undisturbed. I knew the ascent of the two old men was not what he expected. Maybe he doesn't have control of everything.

While I've been sitting here, I've noticed some red bumps like pimples slowly covering my skin. Scratching does not relieve the growing irritation. It could be an allergic reaction to something, but I do not have any known allergies. I hope it's not some disease I picked up on the street because of those two old men.

The group of ten young men walked through the busy main street of Petra. Timothy clutched his Bible tightly to his chest, praying fervently for God's grace and protection. He knew the other nine men were praying, as well as the believers back home. No one knew what to expect.

Over a month ago, the Lord gave several of the new converts a desire to preach to all of Petra. They began to go onto the streets and business areas stopping people and asking the passers by if they would be interested in discussing the Bible. Most just shook their heads and kept going, but a few listened and even accepted the Messiah, the Lord, Jesus Christ. With that small bit of encouragement, the new converts sought the elders advice on more effective witnessing. In a few weeks, a group of ten young men led by Timothy formed with the purpose of preaching to a crowd. They already knew of other Believers who had attempted to preach but were out shouted by the orthodox leaders and bombarded by rocks. The elders felt a unified prayer group, with so many young man eager to spread the gospel of the coming King, could have very fruitful results. Almost forty people stayed behind to pray continuously while the young men set out on the mission.

Timothy stepped onto the rocky ledge near the entrance by which he first came into Petra. The other nine spread out around him, ready to help anyone who might truly be interested on the gospel, or intervene if a mocker tried to disturb the preaching.

Noticeably shaky, Timothy started by calling out for all Israel to hear. Men, women and children stopped and drew closer to listen to the brave young man. As over fifty people gathered with more closing in, Timothy felt an unusual calming over him. The words seemed to flow in the Hebrew language.

"I am a Russian immigrant to Petra from Jerusalem. I lost my brother and sister to the wicked cruelty of the King. I have known no other type of life, but of persecution. I wondered how God could allow such a life to someone of His chosen race. I thought God was to rule from our regathered country and we would be exalted to our righteous place on earth."

Two hundred gathered with more by the minute to listen, with hundreds of others hearing the message due to the echoing effect from the rock walls.

Timothy paused for a moment then continued, "The Scripture has concluded that Israel will hold the throne of the coming Messiah. Isaiah, Jeremiah, Zechariah, Malachi and the others promised the Messiah and His coming Kingdom. With the wicked King's slaughter of our people and his takeover of our land, does it mean the Scriptures are wrong? Will we die in this wilderness? Has our God forgotten us?"

Again, Timothy paused. Hundreds more stopped to listen. The traders in the area quit bargaining, no one could pass through the small passageway. All ears were attentive to the young man preaching about God.

"No, my friends, God has not forsaken us. Did God forsake us when Moses led our people into the wilderness? No, we had refused to believe the promise. Did God forsake us when Nebuchadnezzar carried our people to Babylon? No, we had refused to believe in the warnings of Scripture. Did God forsake us when the Romans trampled our country into oblivion? No, we had refused the promise of the Holy One. Has God forsaken us now? I am here to tell you the Scriptures predicted this time and the Messiah is coming as God promised.

Daniel predicted this time in our history. That Satan would defile the temple. Ezekiel predicted Russia's attempted slaughter and their ultimate demise. Zechariah, Daniel and others predicted the Wicked One who now seeks to destroy all of our people from earth. Even our hiding place here in Petra, is predicted in the law for those who have unwillingly committed murder. Whom have we murdered you ask? Our fathers murdered the prophets that God sent in times of old. They disobeyed God's voice time and time again. Finally, they rejected God's only Son, the Messiah, and God used the Romans to obliterate our nation until the times of the Gentiles would be finished.

We now stand on the threshold of that time. The Messiah is coming to bring in the new Kingdom. The Scripture says, *And then the sign of the Son of Man will appear in the sky, and then all the tribes of the earth will mourn and they will see the Son of Man coming on the clouds of the sky with power and the great glory.* The only man who can rightfully take His place as our King, the one who fulfilled all prophecies and righteousness. The Holy One who was resurrected to save us from the evil one, is none other than Jesus Christ, the Son of David."

Immediately a great tumult erupted. Stones began to fly as some people screamed, "Away with him! Rebel! Blasphemer!"

Timothy tried to continue his preaching but a large stone struck his jaw, throwing him off balance. Another stone cracked his knee and he fell to the ground in pain.

Fighting broke out between those who wanted to hear more, and those screaming obscenities. The other young men with Timothy tried to find those who were interested, to give them information for meetings, but everyone became entangled with the ensuing riot.

Within minutes, soldiers fired bullets into the air as they marched into the middle of the fist fights. Timothy was pointed out and a group of four soldiers surrounded him. A captain took the ledge where Timothy had been and announced the end of the tumult. Reluctantly, the incensed crowd dispersed to the normalcies of daily routine, while Timothy was carried off to army headquarters with blood rolling down his cheek and leg.

Day 2070

The King methodically tapped his index finger on his desk. The news of all the rivers transformed to blood blared from the television. He was noticeably irritated at the event, though he had prepared wonderfully. For the last couple years, storage bins for water were constructed near all his offices and properties. Similarly, six years ago, he built bins and freezers to store enough food to last at least seven years. Which is why we continue to eat so well while the rest of the world is starving. The King promised to take care of me if I would give seven years to Him. The way I figure, it's just one of the perks I deserve for this job.

Then, three months ago, all the seas and oceans became blood, killing all marine life in them and diminishing our water sources. Today all rivers and springs turned to blood, which probably will result in ending the earth's water supply.

After listening to the broadcast, the King buzzed for his media director, "Make it known that I am deeply saddened by this latest attempt of the God of the Jews to hurt our environment." He related to the director, "It is obvious He cares nothing for animals, people or our world. We will take every measure possible to undo the evil brought upon us. We shall prevail."

I listened to the King's words of sadness and heartfelt displeasure. His genuine love of mother nature drastically countered the wicked God of the Jew's hatred of all mankind.

The battle rages with many innocent casualties. My anger rises every time I think of the time required to right all the wrongs caused by our enemy. Isn't it amazing how quickly evil destroys, while forces of good can only try to prevent the cancerous spreading? As the saying goes, "Rome wasn't built in a day, but it was destroyed in a day."

Jacob and Timothy walked casually down the valley away from the heat of Petra enjoying the blooming flowers and sights on the valley. Timothy stopped to pick some dates from off one of the many fruit trees and handed some to his father. "Dad, do you think there is any chance that Natasha or Paul may still be alive?"

Jacob stopped and looked up into the heavens. A small smile crept across his face as he answered, "I guess it really doesn't matter either way, we won't see them until after Armageddon whether they are alive or with the Lord. I suppose I have just given over to the fact that they are in the comfort of Jesus' arms, and that's better than being out there under Satan's reign."

"But don't you miss them?" Timothy asked.

Jacob turned back to his son, "Of course I do. I think about them every day. But I know I will see them next year."

Both paused for a moment, remembering Paul and Natasha. Jacob turned back towards their home looking down as he kicked a pebble down the path. "Timothy, I'm not very good about expressing my feelings, especially towards you."

"It's okay, Dad, I..." Timothy tried to interrupt.

"But I am very proud of you. Several times you were almost killed because of your boldness for Jesus Christ. I even cried when I was praying about your preaching, because I don't want to be here without you. Yet, I am as joyous as any father would be when I watch you teaching Bible study or walking off to preach in the streets. I remember before we accepted Jesus as our Messiah, that I wanted you to be successful in the world. I was so worried about you failing and you seemed to be disinterested in family affairs or making good grades. Now look at what God has done with you. All those worldly things are gone and here you are earning riches in Heaven. What greater joy could any father hope for? Next to your mom, you are the biggest blessing in my life. I wouldn't trade you for anyone or anything."

Jacob stretched his arm across Timothy's shoulders and pulled him next to his side. They walked back in silence, smiling as both dreamed of the coming day of the Lord's return.

Day 2250

The King shouted into the phone, "We have less than a year to have everything ready. I don't care how much they hate the heat, we need more weapons. We must defeat the enemy and His army."

I don't pay much attention anymore to his many conversations of weapon and troop build ups. With the temperature close to a hundred in the building, I'm already dripping sweat without the extra effort. If I move at all, my clothes scratch the sores covering my body and the salt from my sweat burns the wounds even more. I'm just glad we have the best cooling system in the world with technicians continually servicing the air conditioners.

The King and I don't leave His office building unless absolutely needed. Everyone else goes home during daylight hours, returning after the sun sets, but the King must do business twenty four hours a day and resort to naps on the couch. If I need to cool down I'm allowed to go to the basement where the King installed freezers to help drop the temperature.

The secretary spoke through the intercom. "Sir, the oil worker's human relations president is here to see you with the other human resources manager."

"Send him in," came the King's quick and irritable response.

A heavy set, tall man dressed in loose shorts and a tank top entered the King's office, followed by two others dressed in tee-shirts. Under the sweat droplets, the King's symbol stood out on their foreheads. All three bowed slightly in reverence for the King, waiting for his approval.

"You may approach," the King ordered.

"Oh, great King, forever be thy Kingdom. The oil employees are greatly disgruntled with the long hours in the heat. They say they cannot survive these conditions any longer."

"What do they want?" asked the King sarcastically.

"Great King, they would like to work only three hour shifts consisting of two hours each with one hour break to cool down in between," the president expectantly requested.

"Will we still be able to meet production quota?" the King asked. "You know how important it is to have enough fuel for the coming maneuvers. And production has been slipping."

"Sir, I believe we can continue as well, if not better with the extra rest. But, you know we have no control over how much oil is retrievable," the president reasoned.

The King eyed him for a moment, then stood up and walked around his desk. He sat down on the edge and put his finger next to his mouth. "Hmm. Is that all?"

"Well, they would also greatly appreciate some rationed water. They say drinking blood isn't refreshing enough to alleviate the heat."

The King stood up and walked up to the president, staring directly into his eyes. A look of fear quickly spread across the rounded face of the exposed man. I knew what he was going through. The searching of your own soul and mind by the King can be a very traumatic experience.

"How did they get these ideas?" The King asked harshly. "How would they know about any water available? Why would they think that working six hours a night would be sufficient for our oil crisis?"

"Well, I...they..." he nervously stuttered.

"You forgot who you work for!" the King angrily said. "You hoped to gain favor with men, instead of obeying my commands. You fool! I don't accept excuses for failure."

The King thrust his open hand into the man's chest. It struck against the president's sternum, his fingers digging between the man's ribs. The president let out a horrific scream, slumping to the floor. The King looked up at the other manager, who fell to his knees.

"You are now the new human relations president. See to it that production increases with no complaints."

"Yes, your highness," the man whimpered still on his knees.

"You may leave," the King commanded.

We sat down ready to watch the news, when a strange darkness covered the sunshine. The King looked puzzled. He stood up and walked over to the window.

"What time is it?" he asked.

"Noon," I replied.

The secretary spoke through the intercom, "Sir, I have some phone calls from the Presidents who are stating that it is now dark in their countries."

"Well, it seems the enemy wants us to gather our forces in the dark," the King said. "I like darkness better anyway."

Day 2430

Thousands of believers were gathered on the hill below the Rubenstein's home. Everyone silently passed cups of grape juice to each other. When the empty cups were gathered, Jacob stepped up onto a perch where all could see and hear him.

"What a great blessing to have so many Believers gathered in the Lord's name and partake of communion, to show the Lord Jesus' death until He comes. We know there are thousands more who could not come, or did not hear about today's gathering. We also know there are over one and a half million Jews in Petra who still do not know that Jesus is the Blessed One who is coming to save us. I am here to say that we only have ninety days until the Lord Jesus will be coming with power and glory!"

The crowd began cheering loudly. Some people raised their hands to the sky, while others just clapped praising God with one voice. A couple minutes later, the crowd hushed as Jacob continued.

"Since we have gathered so many Believers today for fellowship, I wanted to read some Scripture pertaining to Armageddon. I also want to read some of the latest Federation news that my son, Tim, gathered this morning from Army Headquarters. I have several new releases that state of a large number of soldiers and military vehicles crossing the Euphrates River which dried up 3 months ago. The King is calling all nations to gather. . ."

Our limousine weaved through the dark streets of Jerusalem, escorted by several military vehicles. There were no kids playing in the street, or even walking on the sidewalk. I could barely see the bodies slouched in the door frames, and windows. No one wanted to do anything except try to stay as cool as possible.

"Your fuel allotment," the King said on the telephone, "may only be used for necessary government vehicles and transporting soldiers to Megiddo. If I have another report of misuse, your country will. . ."

The driver stopped the limousine. A building was collapsing into the street in front of our car. I could feel the violent shaking, even though I sat in the most luxurious vehicle in the world.

The King said, "Stay in here. You're safe with me."

Bricks, from a collapsing building, ricocheted off the car window. I was thankful for the bullet proof glass and metal reinforced armor surrounding me.

As the earthquake came to an end, I heard several pellets hitting our roof. Moments later, giant hail balls pounded against our limousine, testing it's strength. I watched the helpless people running back into the destroyed buildings of which they had just fled, trying to escape the beach ball size hail. Those not finding shelter were crushed by the heavenly bombardment.

When the ordeal ended, the King picked up the red-line phone connected directly with General Carlos. "General, what is the Federation status? Well find out and call me back."

The King called for a helicopter to pick us up, because our limo was trapped in by fallen buildings.

The helicopter whisked us towards the airport, as the King continued phone conversations with the world leaders. I pressed against the window, earnestly looking at the fires and the wreckage below. I did not see any building that wasn't damaged, and most were totally ruined.

The airport was in a state of emergency. The earthquake had ripped all the runways into unlandable cement piles. Planes, full of soldiers that were approaching Jerusalem, were now circling above with little fuel remaining.

The King ordered His jet ready and that we would fly out as soon as a runway was ready. We boarded the jet, which was already in position for take off. I heard the intercom warn us of a plane out of fuel and coming down.

"Tell them to land on another runway, or we'll shoot them in front of us," the King demanded. I must get to Babylon immediately.

We started our take off, and I watched two planes attempt landings on the broken airstrips. The first plane never touched the runway as the landing tires caught a mound of rubble. The nose dove into the ground and the tail turned skyward, flipping the plane onto its back in a huge burst of flames. The second plane never put the landing tires down. It skidded over the runway in a fountain of sparks, but stopped in an upright position.

A bright orange glow, illuminated the darkness as we approached Babylon. Fires engulfed the remains of the ruined city. Every building was brought to the ground in the massive earthquake. I saw hundreds of ships with their crews watching from on deck, anchored several miles out in the sea. No one had ever seen such a great city destroyed so quickly and thoroughly.

The King, who had been staring out the plane window in silence, put his head in his hands. He muttered, "Oh, my great city Babylon. You were my pride and joy."

He shook his head in disbelief, then looked up at the ceiling as if someone were there. "You will pay for doing this to me!" he shouted. "Why do you care about this lousy planet, anyway? No one wants you as their God. They have chosen me. They have always chosen me. They rebel against you every chance they get. Look at your chosen people in Petra. They don't know who their Messiah is. How can you love such sinning people? I will discipline them for you, just like in the past. Don't try to stop me. I will kill your Son again if I have to. And this time I have the entire world behind me!"

Day 2512

Our jet landed in Israel's biggest airport, in the valley of Megiddo. The King's limo was waiting to drive us to Haifa for the King's summit meeting. The president of every country in the world was required to be at the final meetings before the Great Victory.

Upon our arrival at the hotel, we immediately went to the banquet hall. All the presidents were waiting in a line for the King's arrival. As we walked in, the entire line bowed down on one knee before us. The King smiled and acknowledged their praise.

"You may be seated," said the King as he stepped up to the podium. "We are gathered here for the next few days to understand my flawless plan in our Great Victory over the Jews, and their evil God. Everyone must follow my plans exactly, or you will face dire consequences."

"First, let me caution you about underestimating the God of the Jews. Though I have defeated Him in the past, He is quite capable of murdering many people during our battle. His cruel and wicked ways have deceived millions throughout the ages. Even now, as He assaults our Mother Earth, His terror victimizes innocent human lives. Your complete worship and following of Me alone, is the only way to finally rid our world of His awful presence."

"Second, thanks to Mother Earth, we have a valley from here through Meggido and directly to Petra. As I speak, Federation soldiers are advancing through the valley to position themselves for the frontal assault in Bozrah Valley. My armies of the world will fill this valley from Bozrah to Meggido."

"After we have positioned all troops and equipment, we will launch an aerial attack first. Then I will lead the greatest army ever assembled, in a ground assault starting in Bozrah. I hope to catch fleeing Jews as they leave Petra from our missile assault. Everyone else must be ready to fight the God of the Jews, if by chance He wants to try to help His people."

"Once the Great Victory is complete, we will assemble in Jerusalem for the largest victory party ever held. Everyone will be given instructions for rebuilding the nations on an equal basis. The God of the Jews will be dead, and I alone will reign as King of earth!"

Day 2516

Tim ran up the dusty path over the rocky hill to his home. Jacob, Sveta and the Solomons were sitting around the stone wall when Tim burst into the family area.

"Federation troops are in Bozrah!" he loudly announced.

"Just where we figured they would be," Jacob answered with a smile, and nodding to Mr. Solomon.

"Exactly sixteen hundred furlongs or one hundred and seventy six miles from Megiddo," Mr. Solomon acknowl-edged, "just like it says in Revelation chapter fourteen."

Tim continued telling his news, "The army is also talking about leaving Petra before the King attacks. But, many of the older people don't think they could outrun the Federation and would rather die here."

"Fools," stated Jacob. "They would have no chance if they left Petra. The Lord has protected us in our city of refuge, why would they want to run now?"

Sveta shook her head and said, "I don't understand why so many people don't realize that our Lord will fight the battle for us."

Mr. Solomon added, "Since so many refuse to acknowledge Jesus as the Messiah, they only have two choices. The Scriptures are wrong and there is no God of the Jews, or the Messiah must miraculously step out from among our people. However, this Messiah still has to fulfil all the prophecies of the Old Testament before He can save us. So they are limited to what they think God can do for them."

"You should see the tens of thousand kneeling in the street and praying towards Jerusalem," Tim stated. "I could barely get from Army Headquarters to here without tripping over somebody."

"Little do they realize who is going to save them, Sveta quipped."

"In Zechariah chapter twelve," Jacob stated, "It says, *all of the delivered remnant will look upon whom they pierced and mourn when they realize who the Messiah is.*"

"Don't forget," Mr. Solomon added, "in Matthew twenty-four, Jesus said all the world will mourn when they see Him coming with power and glory."

Jacob leaned back against the rock wall, and shut his eyes. "Just four more days and we will see Jesus."

The King gave his final instructions and words of encouragement to the Commander. He wanted to hurry to the front line, but a group of national journalists were waiting in another hotel and the King wanted to greet them. Each nation had selected one government person to be the official journalist who would write about the Great Victory. These writings were to be used in future textbooks and official papers.

We walked into the room with bright lights shining into our eyes. The entire group of journalists bowed before the King with many chants of praise for him.

"Please, be seated," the King said in his deep, calming voice. His white uniform, with its many medals of honor covering his chest, glowed from all the lights pointed on the stage. Because of my many years of service, I sometimes forget what a brilliant sight the King is for those who have never seen Him.

The King greeted the room full of journalists with a prepared speech that he repeated in over fifty languages. The audience stood for a standing ovation as the King ended with, "Death to the God of the Jews."

Each national representative was allowed to give praise to the King and shake His hand. They pushed each one through at a rapid pace, but the King took a moment with the United States representative. I think he wanted to search the man's soul for any sign of disobedience. After the last one filed past, we hurried to the waiting helicopter for our flight to Bozrah.

Once in the limousine, the King looked directly into my eyes. "Joseph," he began with a deep seriousness in his voice, "you have done a tremendous job for me over these last seven years. You have also been treated like a king as I promised. However, your task is not complete. The greatest challenge is still before you."

He leaned forward and continued, "You have been given a power like no other human. This power must be used to defend my life in the battle to come. If the enemy tries to retaliate our force, he will focus on hurting me. You and the other bodyguards must remain totally attentive to protecting my life and shielding me from any vengeance of the enemy. Though I don't foresee any problems, our enemy is very wicked and crafty. He is capable of almost anything."

The King looked directly into my soul, as though he were not talking to me. "Do you understand?" He spoke in a deep voice.

I felt a power surge from within my inner being. It flowed up my throat and over my tongue. I spoke in a raspy voice, I wasn't sure was mine, "Yes, your Highness."

"Good," the King replied leaning back in the seat. "Have you thought about where your new mansion will be?"

Stuttering, as if I had just come out of a trance, I replied, "I had not thought about it, Sir."

"Don't worry," he replied with a smile, "there will be plenty of time to think, after the battle."

Day 2520

The King sat silently in the helicopter as we flew to our appointed place by the front line. He gazed out the window inspecting the positions of the military below. The Great Prophet sat across from us, with his eyes closed in deep meditation. I sat next to the King fidgeting with my guns and bullet-proof vest.

I could not help but to think that this might be my last day. The words of the King's orders echoed through my head. Our enemy is wicked and crafty, He might even dare to attack our army. If He attempts to harm my King, I knew out of instinct, that I would give my life for my lord. It would be the highest honor any man could hope for.

I adjusted my helmet and checked the radio transmitter. I was nervous. The thought of not being at the Great Victory party bothered me. Would anyone remember me with a moment of silence? I worked very hard for these last seven years to earn a mansion and retirement anywhere in the world. Will it all come to an end, today?

Tim sat at the entrance of their home, looking towards the darkness in the distance. He tried to imagine what the world troops were doing to prepare for the battle. Do they really believe they can win? How soon would they begin to attack? When would Jesus come to save us?

"Hi, Son," Jacob interrupted his thoughts. "Did you sleep last night?"

"No," answered Tim, turning to see his father. Even with all the problems and stress of the last three and a half years, his father seemed almost younger than before. He always smiled an gave words of encouragement to the family, friends and even those who persecuted his faith in Jesus Christ. The Lord really changed him. "I was too excited to sleep."

"Me, too," laughed Jacob. He looked at Tim with a smile. He had grown up from the rebellious teenager he used to be. No more complaints or fits of anger when problems crossed his path, just a peaceful and joyful attitude. All the Believers admired his firm stand for Jesus Christ, and his willingness to suffer persecution because of it. He had become a man of God.

"Up early?" Sveta asked, walking out to join her husband and son.

They looked down at the enormous gathering of Jews praying towards Jerusalem for deliverance. "Will we see Paul and Natasha, today?" Tim asked staring back at the darkness.

"Yes," Jacob answered, "sometime today, our whole family will be together in the presence of our Lord Jesus."

Jacob put his arms around his wife and son. Then he began to pray.

The helicopter landed next to the King's tower, built for Him to command and watch the Great Victory. We ascended up the steps to the control room, three hundred feet above the army below. The King took His position at the helm, looking down on the valley lit by millions of torches,

"Is everything prepared and ready to begin?" the King asked General Carlos.

"Yes, your Highness."

"Scramble all fighter jets," the King ordered.

"Yes, Sir," General Carlos answered with a short bow. He walked to his command center and began the operation.

The King spoke into the microphone connected to thousands of speakers throughout the valley of Megiddo. "The time has come, my children. I will lead us to victory over the Jews and their God. With the best military equipment, nuclear warheads and over one billion soldiers, we will not be defeated. Bow down in worship of me!"

The chants of praise echoed through the valley and up to the King. He raised His hands into the air accepting their worship.

He turned to General Carlos, with fire in His eyes and death in His voice, "Kill the Jews."

The General nodded in obedience and gave the order to the fighter jets.

"Remember," the King exclaimed, "at any sign of the God of the Jews, you must launch all nuclear missiles immediately. Do not hesitate with either the ones pointed at Petra, Jerusalem or in the air. If He shows up, I want to blow Him back to His Heaven."

Every person in Petra sat or kneeled throughout the valley. The army intelligence had announced that the King was in Bozrah and preparing to attack. There was no place to hide or run to. Everyone chose to meet death in the face, rather than cower inside the caves. Their only hope, as they fervently prayed, would be the miraculous coming of the Messiah.

The Rubensteins and Solomons were joined by hundreds of other Believers on the hillside outside their home. They were also praying, but to Jesus Christ and for His promised return.

"Dad," Tim whispered. "Do you have any doubts at all that Jesus won't come."

"Every time a doubt enters my mind," Jacob answered, "I tell myself that the only way I'm wrong is if Jesus lied. Then I just pray to Jesus and say that I have no hope, but Him. I sometimes quote Scripture. Then I just rest in the fact that I know Jesus wasn't a liar."

"Then its okay to doubt?" Tim asked.

"As humans, our flesh will always doubt what we can't see or touch. But, God is not flesh. Hebrews chapter eleven, verse one says, *Now faith is the substance of things hoped for, the evidence of things not seen!* Our faith is not based on how much we believe, but what we believe in."

"I understand, "Tim replied. "The doubts I have are from my flesh, or old nature, before I accepted Jesus. The only way to overcome them is through the evidence in Scriptures and the Holy Spirit which is in me."

"Exactly," answered Jacob. "We are not trusting in any way that we can defeat the Anti-Christ as he attacks us. We may not understand how or why Jesus will save us, but we have fully trusted that He will do what He promised. Our assurance and peace is not from our feelings, but in the Word of God."

"I hear something!" Sveta exclaimed.

The group sat perfectly still, listening to the approaching roar of fighter planes.

"Their coming," Sveta nervously said.

The roar of thousands of jet engines grew closer. Everyone throughout Petra, strained to see into the wall of darkness. In an instant, hundreds of planes broke out of the darkness, immediately launching the missile attack.

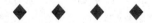

We could hear the jets approaching and with a thunderous roar they passed overhead. The King stood, with his hands grasping the control center in front of him, watching the jets fly towards the target.

"Their in the clear and firing now!" the General exclaimed.

A bright light flashed in the sky above us! The darkness is rolling back like a scroll. The light is spreading to the east and west.

"Fire the warheads now!" the King screamed.

A deafening roar pierced into my ears from thousands of missiles launching around us.

The God of the Jews is descending on a white horse. He has a crown and His eyes are as fire. An entire army on white horses is descending behind Him. He is opening His mouth. The missiles are exploding and He is consuming all the power! He's reaching for the King. I must protect him.

I jumped up onto the control board in front of the King. I covered my head with one arm and shot my explosives with the other. Something was tearing apart my inner most being. I could feel the presence inside my body being torn away. I looked up for one brief moment.

I can only see His name. KING OF KINGS AND LORD OF LORDS!

And the beast was taken, and with him the false prophet that wrought miracles before him, with which he deceived them that had received the mark of the beast, and them that worshiped his image. These both were cast alive into the lake of fire burning with brimstone.

And the remnant were slain with the sword of him that sat upon the horse, which sword proceeded out of his mouth: and all the fowls were filled with their flesh.

Jacob saw the planes break through the darkness and fire their missiles. His heart seemed to stop and a lump came into his throat.

A bright flash exploded above him. He looked up to see the glorious white horse descending from the heavens. Jesus' glory was purer than the whitest snow.

The missiles and fighter jets burst into balls of fires, and disintegrated before the cheering Jews. The Messiah had come as He promised.

"Come on, dad," Tim yelled running down the hill, "let's go meet Jesus!"

Jacob grabbed Sveta's hand and followed behind the others. He didn't think about how far they would have to run. It didn't matter. He kept looking up at the Savior descending towards Jerusalem, as the darkness gave way to the light.

The whole valley was filled with excitement, as the Jews ran towards the opening in the mountains created by the last earthquake. It led straight to Jerusalem. Some were shouting others were crying, but no one stayed in their place of refuge anymore. It was time to return to the city of David, where their Savior would reign as King of Kings and Lord of Lords.

Jacob could see the armies of heaven following behind Jesus on their white horses. They were clothed in beautiful robes, reflecting the glory of the Lord. The entire world filled with their brightness. He stopped to wipe the tears from his eyes.

Paul and Natasha descended through the clouds like a dove. Their horses following in perfect order behind the King of Kings.

"It seems like yesterday we were running from the Antichrist," Paul stated.

"Yes," Natasha replied. "I'd already forgotten about earth."

"Three and a half years with Christ," Paul quipped, "would make anyone forget this world."

"Look!" exclaimed Natasha. "I see Tim and Mom and Dad. Dad's stopping to wipe his eyes. He's crying."

"How can you see them amongst two million. . . Oh, there they are," Tim stated. "I see them too. Everything is very clear from here."

And his feet shall stand in that day upon mount of Olives, which is before Jerusalem on the east . . . And the Lord shall be King over all the earth: in that day there shall be one Lord, and his name one.

EPILOGUE

Satan: Just the word conjures vivid images of horror and evil. The one who opposed God and deceived Eve. He roams like a lion, seeking whom he may devour (1 Pet. 5:8). God gives Satan seventeen different names in the King James version.

They are:

1. **Satan** (Job 1:6; Matt. 4:10 and many others)
2. **Devil** (Matt. 25:41; I Peter 5:8 and many others)
3. **Destroyer** (Psalm 17:45; I Cor. 10:10)
4. **Beelzebub** (Matt 10:25)
5. **Dragon** (Rev. 16:13)
6. **Lucifer** (Isaiah 14:12-17)
7. **Serpent** (Gen. 3:1-3; II Cor.11:3; Rev. 12:9-15;Rev. 20:2)
8. **God of this world** (II Cor. 4:4)
9. **Prince of this world** (John 12:31)
10. **Prince of Darkness** (Eph. 6:12)
11. **Assyrian** (Isaiah 10:24; 14:25; Micah 5:5-6)
12. **King of Babylon** (Isaiah 14:4)
13. **King of Tyre** (Ezekiel 27:1-4; 28:12)
14. **Father of lies** (John 8:44)
15. **Accuser** (Rev. 14:12)
16. **Deceiver** (2 John 7)
17. **Tempter** (Matt. 4:3)

Satan in all his pride, tried to mimic God in everything. God sent His Son, Jesus, the true Messiah. Satan will send his son to be the world's messiah. Jesus loved and cared for the world, and even gave His own life to save all who would believe in him. (John 3:15-18). Satan's son will kill and destroy the people of the world. He will demand all of mankind to worship him. This son of Satan is given eleven names in the King James version (some are similar to Satan).

They are:

1. **Assyrian** (Isaiah 10:5-6 and 30:27033)
2. **King of Babylon** (Isaiah 14:4)
3. **Lucifer** (Isaiah 14:12)
4. **Little Horn** (Daniel 7:8; 8:9-12)
5. **King of Fierce Countenance** (Dan. 8:23)
6. **Prince that shall come** (Dan.9:26)
7. **Wilful King** (Dan. 11:36)
8. **Man of Sin** (2 Thess. 2:3)
9. **That wicked** (2 Thess. 2:8)
10. **Antichrist** (1 John 2:18)
11. **Beast** (Rev. 3:1-2)

As there is a holy trinity: God the Father, Jesus the Son, and the Holy Spirit (1 John 5:6-7; Romans 1:4), there will be an unholy trinity: Satan, the Antichrist, and the False Prophet (Rev. 13:11-18; 16:13). The Holy Spirit brings people to Jesus, and the False Prophet will bring people to the Antichrist. The unholy trinity is wickedness incarnate trying to deceive the whole world (Matt. 24:24).

Satan is very powerful and not to be taken lightly (Jude 9). We are not to be afraid of Him (Isaiah 10:24), but realize he can tempt, (Matt. 4:1-10, Gen. 3:1-3), lie, deceive and use all sorts of wicked devices to keep you away from Jesus.

If you have accepted Jesus as your personal Savior, then Satan and his angels will try to keep you from growing in the Lord. God gives many ways in the Bible to defeat sin and Satan.

The chief ones being:

1. **The Word of God** (Matt. 4:1-10; Psalm 17:4-5)
2. **Put on the armor of God and pray** (Eph. 6:11-18)
3. **Resist Satan and submit to God** (James 4:7)

However, if you have not accepted the Lord Jesus as your Savior, you have no power over Satan. He can take you captive, at his will (2 Tim. 2:24-26). He can devour you (1 Peter 5:8). He can destroy you (1 Cor. 10:10), and **he has already deceived you** (2 John 7). How can he do this? He will try to beguile or confuse you about the simple way to Heaven, which is only through faith in Jesus Christ alone (2 Cor.11:3). He will blind you in any way of the world (money, relationships, job, philosophy) to keep you from seeing the beauty of Jesus Christ's love and salvation.

Which God will you choose to believe? The Bible says that Satan will be cast into an eternal lake of fire and brimstone to be tormented forever and ever (Rev. 20:10). Jesus said the lake of fire was specially prepared for Satan and his angels (Matt 25:41). Unfortunately, all who choose to listen to any of Satan's lies will also be cast into the same lake of fire on Judgment Day (Rev. 20:11-15).

Some of these lies include:

1. I believe there is a God.
2. I am trying to be as good as I can.
3. God won't let anyone go to hell.

James 2:19: *Thou believest that there is one God; thou doest well: the devils also believe and tremble.* If believing that God exists was the only requirement, then Satan will be in Heaven with us! Satan knows all about God. Satan has talked face to face with God. Satan also **knows** his end is the lake of fire (Rev. 12:12).

Romans 3:23: *For all have sinned and come short of the glory of God.* If you have ever committed a sin, then you are a sinner! James 2:10: *For whosoever shall keep the whole law, and yet offend in one point, he is guilty of all.* God is perfect. Heaven is perfect.

If you enter as a sinner, it won't be a perfect place. No matter how much you do to gain God's favor (go to church, get baptized, pay money, pray or sit on the ground and beat yourself with a stick), the fact remains, you are a sinner and God cannot allow sin to enter His perfect Heaven.

Many people think that since God is a God of love (1 John 4:8), then He won't send anyone to hell. However, God is a Holy God (Rev. 4:8; Isaiah 6:3; Psalm 145:17), and Holiness will not allow sin in it's presence. If you have sinned or done anything wrong, then you are not holy and deserve to be sent away from God's presence. Romans 6:23a: *For the wages of sin is death.* . .God does not send us to hell, we send ourselves by the sins we commit (Isaiah 64:6-7) Is there any hope? Yes!

Just as you can choose Satan and eternal death whether by his lies, deception or ignorance, you can also choose the Lord and eternal life. God is a God of love, and He does not want anyone to go to hell! 2 Peter 3:9). However, you must come to God on His terms. He has laid out clearly in the Bible. They are:

1. **Realize you are a sinner!** (Romans 3:10, 23; Psalm 38:8; James 2:10)
2. **Realize you cannot obtain God's favor by trying to do good works** (Isaiah 64:6-7; Eph. 2:8-9) **and you deserve punishment, which is eternal death with Satan and his angels.**
3. **A payment is required for your sins.** (Romans 6:23; Psalm 32:1; Isaiah 53:10)
4. **Accept the payment as offered.** (Eph. 3:8-9; John 14:5-6; Isaiah 53:6)

HERE'S THE GOOD NEWS: SALVATION IS FREE FOR YOU! Ephesians 2:8-9: *For by grace are you saved through faith, and that not of ourselves, it is the gift of God, not of works, lest any man should boast.* Romans 6:23b: *But, the gift of God is eternal life through Jesus Christ our Lord.* Yes, God is offering you the greatest gift you could ever receive. But it was purchased at an awful cost. That cost was the life of Jesus, His Son.

God knew that you could not obtain favor, nor fellowship with Him because of your sins. But, He loves you and doesn't want you to perish. The only way to allow you into Heaven, was to pay for your sin. He sent Jesus to earth and Jesus lived a perfect, sinless life (2 Cor. 5:21). Because Jesus was perfect, He could take the wrath of God for you, in your place. He allowed Himself to be beaten, whipped, totally humiliated and hung on a cross. Then, while your sin was placed upon Jesus, God the Father had to turn His back. His holiness separated Him from His own Son because of the sin Jesus paid for. Finally, Jesus took His own life back, resurrected Himself to prove His deity and show that you can live forever in Him!

That is history and Biblical. Today, right now, you must make a choice. Accept the payment a loving God is offering to you for free, or follow in the footsteps of Satan. Revelation 20:15: *And whosoever was not written in the book of life, was cast into the lake of fire.* The only way to be written in the book of life, is to have eternal life: *This life is in his Son* (1 John 5:11); *I am the way, the truth and the life, no man comes to the Father, but by me.* (John 14:6); *Verily, verily, I say unto you, He that believeth on me hath everlasting life. I am that bread of life* (John 6:47-48).

Jesus Christ is standing at the door of your heart (Rev. 3:20). Will you believe in Jesus and the payment he made as your only way to reach Heaven? If you are willing to trust in Jesus for your eternal life, He will come into you and you will possess the bread of life. Praise God!

There is nothing more to accepting Jesus as your personal Savior. Is it really that simple? Yes, and Satan will do everything in his power for you to be corrupted from the simplicity that is in Christ (2 Cor. 11:3).

I encourage you to tell someone of your new life, or of your renewed commitment to Christ. Whoever gave you this book can probably help and encourage you, or please write to us at:

The Prophetic Word
P.O. Box 867
Wentzville, MO 63385

SCRIPTURE STUDY ON THE ANTICHRIST

Daniel 7:8, 9, 20-22, 24-25
Daniel 8:9-12, 23-25
Daniel 11:36-12:1
2 Thessalonians 2:4, 9-10
Revelation 13:2-8

Other Notable Scriptures

Isaiah 10:5-27
Isaiah 14:9-11
Daniel 9:26-27
1 John 2:18
Ezekiel 27:1-4
Ezekiel 28:2-5, 12
Revelation 12:1-13:1
Hebrews 2:14

Bible Prophecies Fulfilled

1. 1930s   Evolution accepted instead of creation (2 Pet. 3:3-7)
2. 1940   World War 1I- the *entire* world at war (Matt. 24:7)
3. 1945   Nuclear weapon (2 Pet. 3:10)
4. 1948   Israel becomes a nation (Matt. 24:32-36; Zech. 14; Ezek. 36,37 and many more)
5. 1948   Israel as one nation (not two) (Ezek. 37:15-28)
6. 1948   Iran opposes Israel (Ezek. 38:4-6)
7. 1948   Iraq opposes Israel (Ezel. 38:4-6)
8. 1950s   Rainy season twice a year (Hos. 6:3; Joel 2:23)
9. 1950s   Russia opposes Israel (Ezek. 38-39)
10. 1950s   Russia becomes a world power (Ezek. 38-39)
11. 1950s   Turkey allies with Russia and opposes Israel (Ezek. 38:4-6)
12. 1950s   Satellite television (Rev. 11:8-9)
13. 1950s   Military rockets are gas powered (Nah. 2:3-4)
14. 1960s   Widespread air travel (Dan. 12:4; Amos 8:12)
15. 1960s   Computers (Dan. 12:4; Rev. 13:16-17)
16. 1960s   Neutron bomb (Zech. 14:12)
17. 1973   Golan Heights becomes a part of Israel (Jer. 50:19)
18. 1973   Carmel becomes part of Israel (Jer. 50:19)
19. 1973   Jerusalem becomes part of Israel (Zech. 14:12)

20. 1970s   "Me first" attitude (2 Tim. 3:1-5)
21. 1984   Oil found in Israel at the foot of Asher (Deut. 33:24)
22. 1984   Oil wells and rigs in Asher (Deut. 33:25)
23. 1986   Libya allies with Russia and opposes Israel (Ezek. 38:4-6)
24. 1988   Ethiopia allies with Russia and opposes Israel (Ezek. 38:4-6)
25. 1988   Iran and Iraq make peace (Ezek. 38:4-6)
26. 1989   Canal built between the Mediterranean and Dead Sea (Ezek. 47:6-8)
27. 1980s   Roses blossom in Israel (Isa. 35:1)
28. 1980s   Israel fills the world with produce (Isa.27:6)
29. 1980s   Israel has up to seven harvests a year (Amos 9:13)
30. 1980s   Barren wasteland becomes fruitful (Ezek. 36:35)
31. 1980s   Hebrew becomes the official language (Zeph. 3:9)
32. 1980s   The shekel becomes the monetary system (Ezek. 45:12)
33. 1980s   Jericho built from refuse (Amos 9:13-14; Ezek. 36:35)
34. 1980s   Nazareth built from refuse (Amos 9: 13-14; Ezek. 36:35)
35. 1980s   Ashkelon rebuilt (Zeph. 2:4;Amos 9:13-14; Ezek. 36:35)
36. 1980s   Ashdod rebuilt (Zeph. 2:4; Amos 9:13-14; Ezek. 36:35)
37. 1980s   Egypt allies with Russia and opposes Israel (Ezek. 38:4-6)
38. 1980s   U.S. questions Russia and backs Israel (Ezek. 38:13)
39. 1980s   England questions Russia and backs Israel (Ezek. 38:13)

40.	1980s	Canada questions Russia and backs Israel (Ezek. 38:13)
41.	1980s	Churches seek pleasure and money (2Tim. 3:4-6)
42.	1980s	Earthquakes (Matt. 24:7)
43.	1980s	Famines worldwide (Matt. 24:7)
44.	1980s	Pestilences: AIDS, cancer, venereal diseases, etc. (Matt. 24:7)
45.	1990	Germany united (Ezek. 38:6)
46.	1991	Many nations oppose Iraq (old Babylon) (Jer. 50:9,41)
47.	1991	Missiles will be perfectly shot (Jer. 50:9)
48.	1991	Hussein becomes afraid (Jer. 50:43)
49.	1991	Iraq's elite guard refuses to fight (Jer. 51: 30)
50.	1991	All nations hear of Iraq's fall (Jer. 50:46)
51.	1991	Iraq filled with men shouting against it (Jer. 51:14)
52.	1991	Foreign troops in Middle East (Isa. 13:4-5; Rev. 19)
53.	1990s	Jews flee from Russia to Israel (Zech. 2:6)
54.	1990s	Jews flock back to their homeland (Ezek. 36,37; Zech. 14; Amos, and many others)
55.	1990s	Different wars all over the world (Matt. 24:7)
56.	1990s	World dependent on Middle East for oil (Jer. 51:7)
57.	1990s	Debit cards (Rev. 13:16-17)
58.	1990s	Scoffers at second coming of Jesus Christ (2 Pet. 3:3)
59.	1990s	Many claim to be "Christ" (Matt. 24:5)
60.	Present	Israel a world power with a great army (Ezek. 37:10)
61.	Present	Israel has not, nor will have, a famine (Ezek. 36:29-30)

62. Present   Israel will never be destroyed again (Matt. 24:32-36; Zech. 14; Ezek. 36-37 and many others)

63. Present   Many fowl(birds) gather in Megiddo (Rev. 19:17; Ezek. 39:17-20)

64. Present   Pause in time before the final elimination (Jer. 51:33)

65. Present   Forming of ten nations in Europe (Dan. 2:26-45; 7:1-28: Rev. 13:1; 17:1-18)

66. Present   One-world government (Daniel and Revelation)

67. Present   One-world bank (Rev. 13:16-17)

68. Present   One-world religion (Rev. 17)

69. Present   Peace Treaty with PLO, Sept. 13, 1993 (Daniel 9:27)

70. Present   Israel preparing for sacrifices again (Hosea 3:4)

71. Present   Conflict in Chechnya with Russia, Iran and Turkey as key nations (Ezekiel 38:2-6)

72. Present   Technology available for personal ID (Rev 13:16-18)

73. Present   Technology available to give life to an image such as in digital animation (Rev 13:15)

To obtain additional copies, return the form below.
↓ ↓